Especially for

....

From

....

Date

....

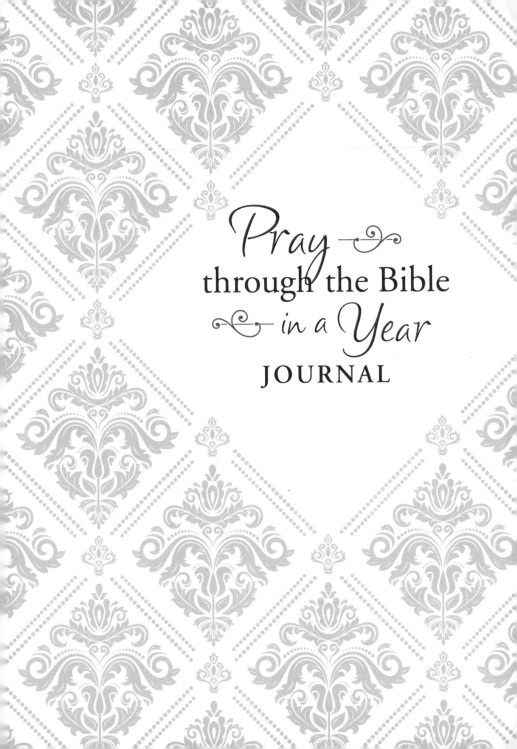

Pray through the Bible in a Year

JOURNAL

Published by Barbour Books, an imprint of Barbour Publishing, Inc., 1810 Barbour Drive, Uhrichsville, Ohio 44683, www.barbourbooks.com

Our mission is to inspire the world with the life-changing message of the Bible.

 Member of the
Evangelical Christian
Publishers Association

Printed in China.

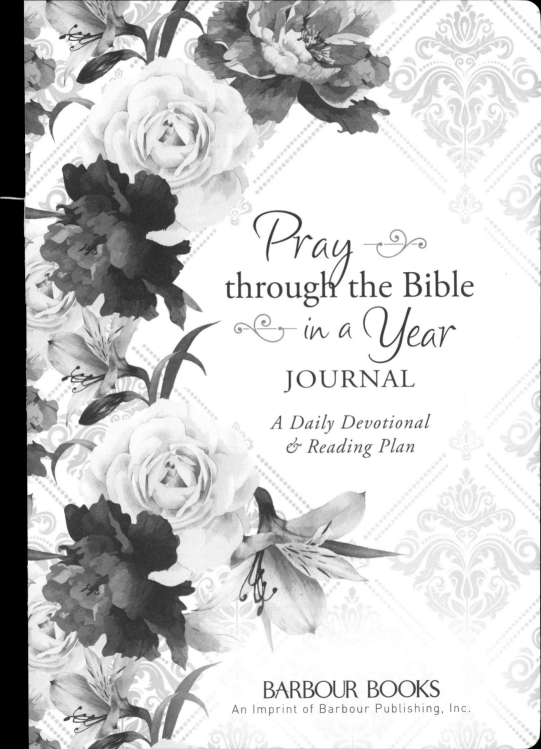

Pray
through the Bible
in a *Year*
JOURNAL

A Daily Devotional
& Reading Plan

BARBOUR BOOKS
An Imprint of Barbour Publishing, Inc.

Introduction

How could one man endure continual persecution and display joy in a prison cell? The answer: prayer. The apostle Paul exemplified the need and power of meditative prayer. His passion for God's Word drove his prayer life. "All Scripture is God-breathed and is useful for teaching, rebuking, correcting and training in righteousness" (2 Timothy 3:16 NIV). Prayer is an essential tool for every Christian's tool kit.

Centuries before Paul, King David rhapsodized about God's Word. In Psalm 19, he described it as worth more than gold and tastier than honey. Almost two hundred couplets in Psalm 119 expand on how and why to dwell in the Bible. It's no wonder that so many people have found the Psalms to be their ultimate prayer-and-song book.

Moreover, God commanded the people of Israel to wrap their hearts and lives around His words. "Talk about them when you sit at home and when you walk along the road, when you lie down and when you get up" (Deuteronomy 6:7 NIV).

What does all that have to do with a book on praying through the Bible? Put it this way. The more a person dives into God's Word, the easier he will find it to pray. Start with praise, then thanksgiving, confession, and praying for yourself and others.

Do you find yourself glorifying God for the same things? Try reading Psalms, the Prophets, and the Gospels. In them, you'll find God's limitless qualities worthy of celebration.

Do you want to thank God for more than your provisions? Find more reasons in the Bible.

Do you sense there are hidden and unknown sins you need to confess? See yourself in the mirror of the law.

Do you wonder how to best pray for yourself? *What does God want from me, and what should I pray for?* Again, God's Word will show you.

Do you struggle with self-absorbed prayer? Perhaps you always pray for the same people. The pages of scripture can help.

When you fill your mind with God's Word, intimate communication with Him becomes the natural result. Use this book to develop the habit of prayer.

All Creation Sings
(Genesis 1)

Creator God, how often You speak to me in the beauty of Your creation. I see Your eternal nature and power in the mountains. I hear Your peace and presence in the sound of waves upon the shore. I feel Your love and delight in the soft fur of a kitten purring against my hand. They prepare my soul for that personal encounter with You in scripture and in Your Son, the Word of God. I pray for those who have deafened themselves to Your voice in creation, that You will open their eyes to the truth by whatever means necessary, before it is too late. Amen.

Day 2

Following God's Dreams
(MATTHEW 2)

GENESIS 3–4

MATTHEW 2

PSALM 2

Wonderful Counselor, I confess I have a lot to learn about staying still, emptying my mind of diversions so I'm ready to listen. I thank You that I hear Your voice as I meditate on Your Word. There are times I would like to have clear-cut directions like Joseph received in his dreams. But You know my heart. Would I be afraid? Am I committed to the unwavering, immediate obedience that Joseph practiced? How I thank You that You know the path my life will take and You are already preparing me. Tune my spirit to the frequency You wish me to listen to. Amen.

As I Awake
(PSALM 3)

Day 3

GENESIS 5–7
MATTHEW 3
PSALM 3

*O*h God who never sleeps, I awake this morning because You sustained me during the night. Today is a gift from Your hand. May I treat it with awe and care, treasuring each moment. May I stay on the path You have laid before me, even when I encounter obstacles. Whatever problems arise today, show me how to glorify You. If I become weak and battle weary, You will lift my head. You are my shield, my deliverer, even when You allow the enemy to assail me. I will lie down tonight, able to rest because You are always with me. Amen.

Day 4

GENESIS 8–10

MATTHEW 4

PSALM 4

Speechless Prayer
(GENESIS 8:21–22)

*R*ainbow Covenant God, I read about Noah after the flood and wonder about his prayers. What did he say to You when he offered clean animals on the altar? Only You know, and whatever words he used, You addressed his greatest needs: safety, food, and repopulating the earth. How I thank You that You understand my heart and my greatest needs. You know my every thought, for good or evil; You know the fears that plague me. And You provide for those weaknesses, sometimes before I ask. Oh God, how can I not want to follow a God like that? Amen.

Going Your Way
(PSALM 5)

Lord God, I look forward to meeting with You every day. I lay my requests before You with full confidence, counting on Your protection. Teach me Your joy in the midst of scary circumstances. Your favor is more than a blessing; it's also a shield against the enemy. Oh, what peace to know that the only harm that comes my way is permitted by You. Lead me on a righteous path. Teach me to love You first and most, and then to love others as I want to be loved. My vision and understanding blur; make Your way straight before me so that I will follow Your path even when the eyes of my heart don't see it. Amen.

Day 6

Praying Is Loving
(MATTHEW 5:44)

GENESIS 14–16
MATTHEW 5:21–48
PSALM 6

Sovereign Lord, I confess I don't like Your command to love my enemies, whether they are personal enemies, nations at war, or religious persecutors. I don't wish them well any more than Jonah wanted good to come to Nineveh. But *pray* and *love* are verbs, actions You command I take no matter what I'm feeling. And You know what happens when I pray for my adversaries. My feelings will change. So as I pray for them, I ask for eyes to see them as *You* see them. And if they walk according to Your will, my life will be better. That's the reconciliation I want. Let me pray in obedience, trusting You with the outcome. Amen.

"What If" Prayer
(GENESIS 18:22–32)

I have to give Abraham credit, Lord. He spoke with You face-to-face and didn't back down. He kept at it, pleading with You to spare Sodom if You could find—in the end—only ten righteous people in the city. He went with a quarter cup–sized request to a gallon-sized, and You kept saying yes. You have done the same for me. I asked for a quarter cup of blessing when You were ready to pour out a gallon. Expand me, prepare me to receive that immeasurable "Yes" when I pray on behalf of others. Amen.

What Is Man?
(PSALM 8)

*L*ord God, this psalm brings the music and lyrics of praise songs to mind. I'm ready to stand with my hands raised to You. At the same time, I'm ready to fall to my knees. *What is man that You are mindful of him? What is woman that You are mindful of* me? When I wait at the foot of the tallest mountain, at the edge of the ocean, on the rim of a volcano creating new land, I feel so insignificant. But the truth is, You made me only a little lower than the angels—crowned with glory and honor, given control over Your creation. I don't understand why or how, but I rejoice in it, praying that all glory will be returned to You. Amen.

Ask, Seek, Knock

(MATTHEW 7:7–11)

Day 9

GENESIS 21–23
MATTHEW 7:1–11
PSALM 9:1–8

Oh heavenly Father, I'm the child from the parable; You are the Father who will give good gifts to Your children when we ask You. When I ask for help from You, it's as scary—and as easy—as asking my earthly father. You may not give me what I ask for, but You will give me what is best. I may knock on Your door, asking You to end a specific war. Instead, You give me Yourself, the Prince of Peace, dwelling in me and one day ruling the world. You give me the answer to what I seek, not the means I think is best. And how I thank You that Your wisdom knows the difference. Amen!

Day 10

GENESIS 24

MATTHEW 7:12–29

PSALM 9:9–20

Because I Know Your Name

(PSALM 9:10)

Jesus, Name above all names, I come to You in faith. You will never forsake me, and there is no one more powerful than You. Your names showcase all the ways You supply my every need. Emmanuel—You are with me every second of my day. Prince of Peace—I rely on You because the road is often bumpy. Wonderful Counselor—I seek You when I don't know which way to turn. You are my all in all. You are King of kings and Lord of lords. I bow before You. Strike even more awe into my heart. You are my all in all. Amen.

When Men and Women Pray

(GENESIS 25:21–23)

Lord, You've heard parents pray for their children since Eve gave birth to Cain. How precious is this record of faith on the part of Isaac *and* Rebekah, the essential link between Abraham and Jacob. How different the prayers of this couple, and what a reminder of the differing roles father and mother bear. Yet You answered their prayers equally. You gave Isaac measurable affirmation—he received a son. You gave Rebekah insight into the twins she carried. Today when I pray, You answer the needs of my mind, soul, and spirit as well as of my body. Amen.

Day 12

Expecting the Unexpected
(MATTHEW 8:23–27)

GENESIS 27:1–28:9

MATTHEW 8:18–34

PSALM 10:12–18

God of the unexpected, how often You surprise me. You always act in accordance with Your character, but not always as I foresee. Often I repeat an ordinary activity, like the disciples crossing the sea of Galilee in a boat. With You by my side, I expect clear sailing, but a storm arises instead. Like the disciples, I'm tempted to rail at You for not paying attention. But You want my faith. You are with me, therefore I have no need to be afraid. Sunshine or rain, You keep me safe. Amen.

Groveling Prayer
(MATTHEW 9:20–22)

GENESIS 28:10–29:35
MATTHEW 9
PSALM 11

*L*ord, part of me identifies with the synagogue ruler, his superspiritual position and his worry for his troubled daughter. How many times have I prayed to You about my family, about those dearest to me? But perhaps I relate even more with the woman touching the hem of Your garment. How often have I reached out, feeling unworthy to be in Your company, among Your people, but knowing You cared about me in spite of everything I felt? Oh Lord, what a welcome promise, that You call that desperate plea an act of faith. When You answer my supplication, all praise goes to You. Amen.

Day 14

GENESIS 30:1–31:21

MATTHEW 10:1–15

PSALM 12

When Will God Arise?

(PSALM 12:5)

*L*ord Jehovah, I pour out my heart to You, asking for Your favor, to make me more like You. And in Your grace, You answer. But Lord, give me the eyes and the ears to feel Your heartbeat. David knew what things got Your immediate attention: when the poor are plundered and the needy groan. You keep them safe. Make me an instrument of Your love for them. Your words to me are more valuable than silver. Change the priorities in my heart—from things to people to Your Word. Then I will better know how to pray. Amen.

Words in My Mouth

Day 15

(MATTHEW 10:18–20)

GENESIS 31:22–32:21
MATTHEW 10:16–36
PSALM 13

Jesus, how You must have smiled when I hated speech in high school, knowing the day would come that I would love to speak in front of groups. But I confess I still clam up when I feel uncomfortable. So thank You for this promise. You will give me the words to say when I'm called to account for my love for You—but that doesn't just mean when I face a firing squad. You will give me words when a coworker asks about my faith. You will shield me with Your words if I'm attacked by family and friends dear to me. I pray I will be living in Your words and by Your Word so that they will naturally fall from my lips. Amen.

Day 16

GENESIS 32:22–34:31
MATTHEW 10:37–11:6
PSALM 14

Wrestling with God
(GENESIS 32:22–30)

*L*ord, how often do we talk about wrestling over a problem while forgetting the man who spent a night physically wrestling with You? Jacob had already prayed to You. But You weren't done with him. You came back and wrestled with him all night. He had come so far, but You wanted to help him along. Oh Lord, I don't know if I have ever prayed like that, because I've never been able to stay on my knees for more than an hour (and rarely for an hour). But like Jacob, I have spent vigils when faced with a difficult situation. You battled with me and for me until I was ready for Your blessing—not in making things easier, but in changing me, strengthening me for the task ahead. I need You, Arm-Wrestling God. I won't leave until You bless me. Amen.

Dwelling with God
(Psalm 15)

Lord Jehovah, who wants to dwell in Your sacred tent, never shaken? I do! I want the promise, but the requirements are beyond me. Speaks the truth? Doesn't hurt a neighbor? Keeps an oath even when it hurts? Oh, how grateful I am that righteousness doesn't depend on me. You made me blameless and righteous in Christ. I am holy because of my address, where I dwell in the heavenlies with Christ. You swooped in with one move and carried me off to the ongoing process of making me holy. In fact, I am Your tabernacle. Amen!

GENESIS 35–36
MATTHEW 11:7–24
PSALM 15

Day 18
———— ⁀ ————

GENESIS 37–38
MATTHEW 11:25–30
PSALM 16

Peaceful Nights
(PSALM 16)

*D*ear Lord, how many of Your people struggle with sleepy days and sleepless nights? Why do I keep turning to You at night, pleading for sleep? Because that's my answer. I keep my eyes always on You, putting a lock on my head, that I may not turn to the right or left but only look straight at You. Because You are my Rock, solid, unmoving, I will not be shaken. You make me secure. You provide for my needs. I have no cause to worry. Beyond that, You give me joy and eternal life. In You there is rest. Amen!

Answers Come from God
(GENESIS 40:8)

GENESIS 39–40
MATTHEW 12:1–29
PSALM 17

Sovereign God, I looked forward to reading Joseph's prayers, to learn from this man who trusted You in spite of everything that would have driven most of us away. But I haven't found them yet while reading the Bible. Only hints here and there, like when he spoke with Pharaoh's servants. "Do not interpretations belong to God?" Lord, I want to call on You like that. To pray so naturally, for prayer to so permeate my life, that my walk and conversation will breathe with the time I have spent with You. For apart from You, I have nothing of worth to offer. Amen.

Day 20

————— ∞ —————

GENESIS 41
MATTHEW 12:30–50
PSALM 18:1–15

Heart-Mouth Connection
(MATTHEW 12:34)

*W*onderful Counselor, once again I fall before You, miserable in the way I use my tongue, provoked to self-defense, to anger, ashamed. Oh Lord, it's been a lifelong battle, my default reaction when I feel pressured. I know it's not pleasing to You. I thank You for Your boundless love and provision. I know that You will free me from this sin and that it begins with a heart change. Oh Lord, so fill my heart with Yourself that all that comes from my mouth is the fullness of Your being, Your grace, Your love, Your joy. Only in You. Amen.

Same as Me
(PSALM 18:25–26)

*O*h Living Word, no wonder Your Word cuts the confusing clouds and unveils the real me. Because You come to me where I am. You take the message and frame it with Your faithfulness. You reveal Your blameless character. Your purity shines light on my understanding. If I'm not ready for that spotlight, You will speak to me in braille until my eyes can see. Oh Lord, how I rejoice because You individualize Your lesson plan, giving me Your strengths and turning my weaknesses into glory for Your name. In all I do, let me honor You. Amen.

Day 22

―――――♧―――――

Battle Prayer
(PSALM 18:30–50)

*O*h Lord my Rock, You are not only my place of refuge; You are also my victory. I confess, often I come to You, hoping, pleading for You to head out to battle while I sit on the sidelines. But You call me to put on Your armor and stand beside You in battle. The victory is still all Yours, but You use my hands to beat them, my feet to trample them. You make my arms strong enough to bend bronze. And I shake my head at that one, because with my current health, I couldn't even pick up a bronze bow. I'm standing up for You, Lord, for You are there for me. Amen.

Where the Rubber Hits the Road
(PSALM 19)

Day 23

GENESIS 46:1–47:26
MATTHEW 13:24–43
PSALM 19

*G*od who sees me, Your word is powerful and beautiful and worthy of study. I desire to imprint it on my heart. But all that means nothing if I don't do what it says. Forgive my sins, both intentional and accidental, and line me up ever more closely with the pleasing path of Your law. May I meditate on Your precepts until the words of my mouth are pleasing in Your sight, reflecting my inner spirit. When I am tired, let me seek rest in Your law. When I need wisdom, may I scan its pages. You have given me all the tools I will ever need. Amen.

Day 24

Praying for Grandchildren
(Genesis 48)

GENESIS 47:27–49:28

MATTHEW 13:44–58

PSALM 20

*H*eavenly Father, thank You for the gift of grandchildren. I can only imagine how excited Jacob was to see Joseph's children and to call down Your blessing on them. I pray that I will be as diligent as Jacob in praying for my grandchildren and now even for the great-granddaughter growing in her mother's womb. I thank You for their unity as a family in worship. I plead they will grow into the beauty of the life You have planned for them, men and women of God. I relinquish their futures to You. More than anything else, I want them to know You. Amen.

Walking on Water
(Matthew 14)

GEN. 49:29–EX. 1
MATTHEW 14
PSALM 21

*L*ord Jesus, I want to be like Peter, racing to You across the dancing waves. Of course, to do that, I have to get out of the boat. Forgive me for those times when I hear Your call but hesitate, doubting Your voice and climbing back aboard. You know about the times I've taken a few steps before I glance down at the waves massaging my feet, how that good beginning melts into a soggy middle. How thankful I am that You understand my frailties. You reach out Your hand and lift me up, safe, secure, walking again on Your invisible pathway. Oh Jesus, help me to step out onto the water. Amen.

Day 26

The Burning Bush

(EXODUS 3)

EXODUS 2–3

MATTHEW 15:1–28

PSALM 22:1–21

"I am who I am" (Exodus 3:14 NIV). Do I dare to say Your name aloud? Yet it's the name You gave to Moses. You are the sum of time and of existence. Apart from You, the world would fall apart. I don't expect to see a burning bush today, but let me feel it with my heart. Fill me with that sense of fear, of awe, of wonder at who You are. So wrap me up in Yourself that I will follow You for the rest of my life, no matter what happens, because the great I Am is always with me. Amen.

Catching Compassion
(MATTHEW 15:32–38)

EXODUS 4:1–5:21
MATT. 15:29–16:12
PSALM 22:22–31

Lord Jesus, You know me. You know I'm the last one eating at the table while everyone else cleans up; You know the blinders I wear when it comes to helping. So I pray that You will speak to me directly, the way You did to the disciples. "I have compassion for these people" (Matthew 15:32 NIV). Point to a specific person at a specific time for a specific need. And when You have called, let me never hesitate. Teach me to act immediately, not worrying about the cost. May my heart beat in time with Yours, and may Your love give sight to my eyes. Amen.

Day 28

Journey of Prayer
(Exodus 6:28–7:6)

EXODUS 5:22–7:24
MATTHEW 16:13–28
PSALM 23

*F*ather, I thank You that the Bible shows me the great saints of faith with all their faults. Abraham was able to go years without hearing from You, but not Moses. You even gave him a helper, Aaron. Oh, how I thank You that I don't have to measure up to someone else. You will prepare me uniquely for my calling. If I need repeated instructions, You are happy to guide me. So let me get busy, preparing for the work You have assigned. With the assistants You have given to me, beginning with the Holy Spirit, I will complete the task. Amen.

The King of Glory
(PSALM 24)

*H*eavenly Lord, everything in me and everything in the earth and skies above belongs to You because You are our Creator. I can claim nothing for myself. How I marvel at the miracle of life, from my DNA to the meshing of matter and energy and all the laws You put into place to make them work in an orderly fashion. That is the God I serve, my standard bearer. Of course You are strong and mighty. You could crush all creation with the wave of a single finger, but instead You deal with me in mercy and grace. Come into my life, oh King of Glory. Rule in me. Amen.

Day 30

My Hope

(PSALM 25)

EXODUS 10–11

MATTHEW 17:10–27

PSALM 25

$\mathcal{T}$he reason for my hope: You are God. That says it all, really, because You are all—everything. And Your passion is to be my personal God. Specifically, You are God my Savior. You have saved me. You are sanctifying me now, and one day You will make my salvation complete. With that hope in mind, I pray that You will grant me a teachable spirit. May I check Your GPS before starting on a journey. I depend on You twenty-four hours a day. Thank You that my hope will never fail because You will never fail. So let me carry that hope clutched close to my heart. Amen.

Behold the Lamb
(Exodus 12)

*B*ehold the Lamb who takes away the sin of the world. Music swells in my heart and I fall speechless at Your nail-torn feet. My tears are an offering of praise for Your blood, the bleach that cleansed me from my sins. You defend me at Your Father's side. My faith has found a resting place in You, in Your wounds that plead for me. If You didn't pass over me? I shy away in terrified shudders. You painted heaven's doorposts with Your blood that I might enter in. No matter how many times or how many ways I say it, I remain broken, prostrate on the holy ground of Your sacrifice. Amen.

Walking the Highway
(PSALM 27)

EXODUS 13–14
MATTHEW 18:21–35
PSALM 27

Teach me Your way, Lord. I'm walking it. I thank You for the confidence of knowing that when I reach my destination, I will see how Your arrow made my way straight from beginning to end. You've put me in an army tank that plows my enemies under as I travel under Your orders. Lord, I seek You. I want to play tag, to sit in Your lap, to watch in awe as You conduct kingdom business. Drum this truth into my soul: I will see Your goodness in the land of the living. Whether my steps today take me through battle or play, I rejoice that You are with me forever. Amen.

No One like You

(Exodus 15:11)

Exodus 15–16
Matthew 19:1–15
Psalm 28

*T*here is no God like You. In a world that depends on science more than a god, dazzle us with Your majesty. Leave me awestruck with Your glory as I rest in Your Son and as I explore Your creation. Perform wonders to open a crack in the hearts and minds of those who don't believe in You. Thank You for revealing Yourself, for giving me eyes to see. Continue to improve my spiritual vision, that I may see You more clearly. Whatever You teach me, may I faithfully pass it on to others. Amen.

Day 34

Exodus 17–19
Matthew 19:16–30
Psalm 29

Am I Prepared for Your Answer?

(Matthew 19:16–30)

Lord, I praise You for all the blessings I couldn't have predicted or planned for. You know my heart. I say I want to follow You no matter what, but I fail in completing the task. How precious to You when, like Isaiah, I offer to go. Forgive me when I back down after I count the cost. Let me be gladly willing to give it all, like martyr Jim Elliot. How I rejoice that You give me the strength for today's problems. If the day comes that You ask for my life, I trust You will give me the grace to bear it. Amen.

Joy in the Morning

(PSALM 30)

I exalt You, holy Lord, because You lift me out of the depths and spare me by Your grace. Although I've felt the heat of Your displeasure in the past, and sometimes in my present, Your favor is my future forever. That is why I eagerly await the shout of joy that will follow a night of weeping. Oh, how I wish I could always enjoy Your sunshine, with good weather. But You see my need for rain to bring growth. Through trials, You make me strong. Come foul or fair weather, my joy is in You. Amen.

Day 36

The First Shall Be Last

(MATTHEW 20:26–28)

EXODUS 22–23
MATTHEW 20:20–34
PSALM 31:1–8

*L*ord Jesus, I've never asked to sit at Your side in heaven. But I confess I've desired recognition among my peers. How I wonder at Your patience with me. You're God, and You gave up everything for me. Me, who's no taller than Your fingernail. And yet You welcome me as a sister into Your family, a coheir of all the heavenly blessings! Let me draw my sense of self from You. Use me as Your hands and feet and heart, unafraid to abandon my "position." That's what other people need—You in me, not myself. Amen.

Moving Mountains
(MATTHEW 21:21–22)

EXODUS 24–25
MATTHEW 21:1–27
PSALM 31:9–18

*L*ord Jesus, I tremble at the depth of this promise. You say You'll move mountains if I ask in prayer, believing. My storyteller's brain imagines a rockslide that halts a robbery or opens a road. But what are the mountains in my life? Lord, when I don't get what I ask for, is my faith at fault? Am I asking for the wrong thing? Or am I blind to Your answers? But it's not about me, or my prayer, is it? It's about You! Jump up and down! You, the God of the impossible. You can lift a mountain with a word. Nothing I can ask or imagine is beyond Your capacity to act. Remove the mountain of my disbelief. Amen.

Give Me Oil for My Lamp
(EXODUS 27:20–21)

EXODUS 26–27

MATTHEW 21:28–46

PSALM 31:19–24

*L*ord, I need oil in my lamp. I'm creaky and rusty, my engine complaining when I crank it. I need *You*. Send Your Spirit through my being. Ease the joints to move. May Your light flare up within me. Forgive me for letting my oil supply run dry, like the virgins waiting for the bridegroom. I thank You that Your oil well is bottomless. Fill me, light me, use me to shine Your light to others. Burn away the impurities in my soul so that the light may shine purer. May I come to You daily for renewal. Amen.

An Invitation

(MATTHEW 22:8–10)

EXODUS 28
MATTHEW 22
PSALM 32

*M*y Lord and King, who am I, that You invited me to the wedding banquet of Your Son? But You not only sent the invitation; You also made me worthy. You saved my soul and gave me new clothes of righteousness to wear. All You ask is that I accept Your gift and come and dine freely at Your table. Oh Lord, with all my being I respond, "Yes, I'm coming!" You've stuffed my hands with invitations to give to others on Your behalf. Litter my path with people You want at Your party, and open my hands to spread the news more heartily than any political campaign. Amen.

Day 40

Make Me an Instrument

(PSALM 33:1–3)

EXODUS 29
MATTHEW 23:1–36
PSALM 33:1–12

*H*eavenly Lord, make me a stringed instrument in the heavenly orchestra. Pluck all ten strings of my heart to resonate with harmonious praise to You. Tune me, that nothing about me will strike a discordant note. Bring our music to a crescendo that will thunder down eternity, Your praise filling every nook and cranny of space and time. May our music dance with the stars and resonate with the waters of the deep. How I rejoice that Your song will never end, the theme never changing, because Your plans stand firm forever. Let me rest on the breath of Your spirit like a leaf floating on the wind. Amen.

Your Love, My Hope

I hope in Your unfailing love. Even when my hope falters, Your love doesn't. Your eyes are on me because I hope in You. I wait in hope. You help and shield me. Your unfailing love sustains me. In You I rejoice day and night. When Your holiness demanded an answer to my sin, You sent Your Son to the cross. Oh holy Lord! Since You reached out and took hold of me in that pit, how much more can I trust You with the minutiae of my life? I begin every day with that hope filling my heart. Amen.

Day 42

━━━━━━⌒♥⌒

Exodus 32–33
Matthew 24:29–51
Psalm 34:1–7

Keeping Watch
(Matthew 24:42)

*L*ord of lords and coming King, is today the day? Will You bring me up to meet You in the sky as I'm eating a cheeseburger for lunch? In my deepest heart, am I ready? I rest in the assurance of my salvation. I long for the realization of Your kingdom on earth. But I confess there's a big part of me that clings to my life as it is. I want to meet my great-grandchild and see my granddaughter get married. I also confess that I'm not as active as I should be in inviting others to the party, in encouraging them to prepare for Your return. Forgive me; clear my vision and purpose. Amen.

Starting Over

EXODUS 34:1–35:29
MATTHEW 25:1–13
PSALM 34:8–22

*Y*ou told Moses everything I ever need to know for when You give me a second chance. You are the Lord! You are compassionate and gracious. You are slow to anger and abounding in love and faithfulness. You look for even the smallest sign of faith. You maintain Your love to the thousands—to me. And although You forgive sins, You're also just. How great Your love that Jesus bore the guilt of my sin; how vast the pit for the one who refuses that gift. On the basis of that undeserved favor, I petition You to go with me. Keep me from heading in the wrong direction. Amen.

Day 44

My Contender

(PSALM 35)

EXODUS 35:30–37:29

MATTHEW 25:14–30

PSALM 35:1–8

*O*h Lord my shield, I come to You, asking for You to rise against my enemies. They seek my life. Don't You see them, Lord, when they plot physical harm? Don't You care when they suck joy from me? Why do You let them fight against me? I run to You. Shine Your light on Your billboard declaring I AM YOUR SALVATION. Take up Your shield and armor. Come to my aid. May Your will blow away those who stand against me, like dust. Oh Lord, how I thank You that You rescue so that I can once again praise Your name. Amen.

Exodus 38–39
Matthew 25:31–46
Psalm 35:9–17

My Lord God, I call on You because You are my God. You're my righteousness. Who is like You? You rescue me from poverty. You hold my life precious in Your sight, God, my Lord. I will give You thanks wherever Your people assemble and will shout hallelujah to You among the throngs. I thank You for friends who stand up for me, who encourage me when I'm down, who praise You and rejoice with me when things are well, who mourn with me when I'm struggling. Your righteousness and greatness will be on my tongue all day long. The more I praise You, the less room I leave for worrying and complaining. Amen.

Day 46

Exodus 40
Matthew 26:1–35
Psalm 35:18–28

Anointing at Bethany
(Matthew 26:6–13)

Lord, in these few days, You have brought me face-to-face with You, alone, letting the rest of the world fade away. In that hiding place, may I pour out my most prized possessions with tears. May I lavish You with all the love I'm capable of. My gift is a pale reflection of You, for You are Love. Break me, that the ointment of Your Spirit may flow over me and through me and return to You in worship. When I leave the privacy of our quiet time, may I carry the fragrance of that anointing. Tip me this way and that, that I may sprinkle Your love along the way. Amen.

Saltshaker

(LEVITICUS 2:11–13)

Day 47

LEVITICUS 1–3
MATTHEW 26:36–68
PSALM 36:1–6

Holy Lord, there's a lot I can learn about prayer from the temple offerings. You have forbidden the leaven of sin in my heart. Search me; show me those hidden places. I don't like the process, but I want to grow more like You. I pray also that the salt of Your righteousness will preserve me from sin. That the flavor of Your will may permeate every request I make of You. That the time we spend together will be food to my soul, a daily party time between two friends. I pray that I will dig from Your salt mine, prepared to season the world around me. Amen.

The Case of Peter and Judas
(Matthew 26:69–27:6)

LEVITICUS 4:1–5:13

MATT. 26:69–27:26

PSALM 36:7–12

*L*ord Jesus, on the night You were betrayed, You reached out to the two men who went the furthest in denying You, Peter and Judas. Oh, how my heart grieves with You. How I bathe myself in the wonder of Your love. Too many of our times together hold echoes of Your warnings to Your close friends. Like Peter and like the hymnist, I am prone to wander. Here's my heart—take it, seal it for Your courts above. How I thank You for Your mercy. I pray for those who, like Judas and Peter, lose their way. Correct their steps; lead them back to repentance and right relationship. Starting with me. Amen.

When Words Aren't Enough
(Leviticus 6:1–7)

Day 49

LEVITICUS 5:14–7:21
MATTHEW 27:27–50
PSALM 37:1–6

*H*oly Lord, how I thank You that You stand ready to forgive my sins. My salvation depends on it as well as my ability to live for You. I thank You for this reminder that my sin doesn't only hurt my relationship with You. When it affects someone else—as it so often does—You call me to reconcile with that person. Oh Lord, I'd rather ignore this part! But Jesus repeated this command, vocalizing in human voice what we had heard from Your written voice. Bring me to obedience. Give me the words to say and the courage to approach anyone I have hurt. Amen.

Day 50

LEVITICUS 7:22–8:36

MATTHEW 27:51–66

PSALM 37:7–26

*L*ord God, You made Aaron's ordination for the priesthood a solemn, holy occasion. Do I expect any less when it comes to preparing for the work You have called me to? You have clothed me in the right uniform by Your Spirit and given me the gifts I need to do the work. I come here, reporting for duty. Before I begin, I wait before You, asking Your forgiveness. Fill me with Yourself and with the skills I need, as You did for the men who built the tabernacle. I ask that all I do will bring glory to You. Amen.

Fellow Seekers

(Psalm 37:27–40)

Leviticus 9–10
Matthew 28
Psalm 37:27–40

Oh Lord, my hope is in You alone, but I am not alone in that hope. I thank You for the company of believers, for those who are blameless and upright. May I focus on what is good and noble and peaceable in their behavior instead of finding fault. Teach me as I watch them. And may they also learn from me. Then we will build one another up and not lead one another astray. Guide me in my choice of companions. Weave us together in holiness and love, that the world will know we belong to You. Amen.

Day 52

~~~~~~~~~~~~~~~~~~

LEVITICUS 11–12

MARK 1:1–28

PSALM 38

Something Beautiful
(PSALM 38)

*O*h Lord, You know the depths of my heart, my longings for something powerful and wonderful, my regretful sighing for the realities of daily life. I praise You, the compassionate God, for You will act on my behalf at the right time, in exactly the right way. My life is an open book before You. You know my dreams and my weaknesses. Burn away the evil in me. Line up my longings with Your own. I lift up my hands to You with confidence, knowing I will receive mercy and find the grace to help me. Lord, I call on You, knowing You will answer. Amen.

Praying for the Sick
(LEVITICUS 13)

Day 53

LEVITICUS 13
MARK 1:29–39
PSALM 39

*L*ord, I thank You for Your concern for the sick. Today I pray for those who are physically, mentally, or emotionally disabled. Open my eyes to see them beyond their labels, as individuals created and loved by You. I lift those with afflictions, STDs like AIDS, that I shy away from. Expand my heart to pray and care and help in any way You lead. I pray also for those whose health limits their activities, who rarely leave home. Use my arms and legs as instruments of Your love. I pray for the necessary support they need, for their health, for their daily activities, and for friendship. Amen.

Right Reason, Wrong Choice
(MARK 1:40–45)

LEVITICUS 14
MARK 1:40–2:12
PSALM 40:1–8

*L*ord Jesus, how often I disappoint You like the leper in today's reading. Like him, after You do something miraculous in my life, I fail to follow Your instructions for follow-up care. Oh, forgive me! I can't claim I don't know. You made it clear in my spirit. Forgive me for making myself blind and deaf. Oh Lord, I tremble at the role I play in delaying the delivery of Your good news to those who need to hear. Today, let me take each step at Your direction, to unleash the chain of events and blessings You wish to unfold. Amen.

My New Family
(MARK 3:13–34)

ord Jesus, from the time You created Adam, You recognized he shouldn't be alone. My mind runs through the list of Your heroes, and I can't think of one without another human to stand by them. How I thank You for my birth family, for placing me with people who prayed and dreamed for me. How grateful I am for my grandmother's legacy of faith. But then You called me away from my family, into a team of believers called to Your purpose. May we go at Your bidding, in Your power, lifting one another up in the power of Your Spirit. Amen.

Watch Where You're Going
(LEVITICUS 16:1–3)

LEVITICUS 16–17

MARK 4:1–20

PSALM 41:1–4

Lord God, how I relish the freedom to crawl on Your lap and call You Daddy. But the instructions for the Day of Atonement remind me that I shouldn't take that freedom for granted. How great Your love for me that I can approach Your mercy seat without fear. You have opened my sin-blinded eyes and given me glasses tinted by Your blood. I have access to You day and night; the veil is torn. May I always cleanse myself with confession and shower myself in Your Spirit. Teach me Your holiness, Your transcendence, Your majesty and power, that my love will be empowered by a holy fear. Amen.

This Little Light of Mine
(MARK 4:21–23)

Day 57

LEVITICUS 18–19
MARK 4:21–41
PSALM 41:5–13

*L*ord Jesus, I am light and salt, and You want my light to shine. You reminded Your listeners that people don't put lamps under bowls. But how often do I turn out my light? Sometimes I'm scared of putting myself out there. Other times a false sense of humility, a feeling that I have nothing worthy to offer, holds me back. As I say it, I hear Your voice telling me, "By yourself you have nothing. With Me you have everything you need." You are the oil in my lamp, Your Spirit the light that burns within me. Forgive me when I doubt Your calling that will bring it to pass. Stop me from ever covering up that light. Amen.

Day 58

———∼⟨⟩∼———

LEVITICUS 20

MARK 5

PSALM 42–43

Where Is God?

(PSALM 42)

*O*h soul, where is your God? I thirst for You, Lord, more than deer, or athletes running a marathon, thirst for water. I'm running a spiritual race to find You, but the finish line keeps vanishing. The door between us seems to be closed. I go to church, but I don't hear Your voice. I still put my hope in You. Deep calls to deep. In the furthest reaches of my soul, I am soaked in the waterfalls of Your love. At night, when all I see is dark, I sing a prayer to You, my life, my Rock, the God of my salvation. I put my hope in You, for I will yet praise You, my Savior and my God. Amen.

My Mother's Prayers
(PSALM 44)

Oh Lord, how precious the legacy of my mother's prayers, how deep and consistent they were. Forgive my feelings of superiority, my pride in Bible knowledge and practices. Thank You for Your patience with the shallow things I offer. Teach me to be a living sacrifice, like Mom. May I learn from her how to be faithful in prayer for my expanding family. May I bring my faults to You as openly as she did, begging for Your strength to make me like You. Please, Lord, mold me so that one day my family will look up to me the same way I cherish Mom. Amen.

Day 60

Celebration

(LEVITICUS 23)

LEVITICUS 23–24
MARK 6:14–29
PSALM 45:1–5

*C*reator God, I thank You for the gift of time and seasons, for the joy the changing length of days, cycle of plant growth, and differing weather bring. I'm especially thankful to live in an area that enjoys four seasons. And among the seasons, You have sprinkled holy days worthy of special celebration. Let me not neglect those occasions, or gathering with Your people to worship each week. How I thank You that every day I can praise You because it is a day You made! Even in the silliness of made-up holidays, like National Frappé Day, I thank You. Daily, may I search for reasons to rejoice in You! Amen!

Bread Bowls

(MARK 6:39–44)

LEVITICUS 25
MARK 6:30–56
PSALM 45:6–12

Lord Jesus, what a sight that day on the mountain must have been. Did Your disciples feel outnumbered in that crowd? I've often felt alone in a group of fifty, let alone five thousand men. Instead of coming to You, I've left in search of an answer. Have I missed Your miracles by slipping away early? Forgive me. These people hadn't even prayed for Your provision. You saw the need and acted. How I thank You for all the times You see the need before I do, that You provide before I ask. And when I seek, You send messengers with bowls of bread. Amen.

Day 62

———⁓———

LEVITICUS 26

MARK 7

PSALM 45:13–17

Reward and Punishment
(LEVITICUS 26)

Oh God my Father, I confess I'm uncomfortable with the if-then nature of rewards and punishments, because it sounds like it's all up to me. If I can manage to live a perfect life, I'll receive every blessing available on earth. But that will never happen. You know that better than I do. You know my struggles with perfectionism in the past, and You know the secret yearnings of my heart that I am blind to. But reading it again, Lord, I see that You want my heart; You want my focus on You. Open my ears that I may listen and obey. Let me never use my failures as an excuse to avoid You, for that would be the greatest sin of all. Amen.

Be Still

(PSALM 46:10)

LEVITICUS 27
MARK 8
PSALM 46

*F*ather God, the greatest thing in all my life is knowing You. I hunger for time with You. But I know so little of the art of being still. Teach me the patience of silence so that I may hear You more clearly. Quiet me so that when I speak, others will hear Your voice, not mine. You will be exalted among the nations. You will be exalted in the earth. You will be exalted by the very people who refuse to acknowledge You. I pray that it happens in this age, and not when everyone is forced to their knees before You. Amen.

Day 64

Dancing before God
(PSALM 47)

NUMBERS 1–2
MARK 9:1–13
PSALM 47

*L*ord Most High, David's psalm makes me want to stand up and shout, sing and dance before You. I want to join hands with people around the world, a global hora before You. The skies would resonate with the sound of clapping hands and joyful cries from all nations. Oh Lord, that's the world I want to see, united in praise of You and not at war with one another! I thank You that one day that will be the reality. It's my birthright as Your daughter. Let me blow Your horn, announcing the good news. You are the King. Of Israel. Of the nations. Of me. Amen.

My Firstborn
(Numbers 3:13)

Lord, You couldn't have made it any plainer: "All the firstborn are mine." Open my eyes to understand better what that means. I fall before You in awe that You gave Your own beloved firstborn to save mine. I lift up my child. How grateful I am that he loves You with all his heart. Thank You for Your peace that allows me to release the pains of the past and the concerns of his present and his future to You. Whatever You ask of him—if You ask him to move far away or to serve as a missionary, soldier, police officer, or firefighter—I commit him to You. Give me the courage to let him go, in every way. Amen.

Day 66

Little Children

(MARK 10:13–16)

NUMBERS 4

MARK 10:1–34

PSALM 48:9–14

*H*eavenly Father, I've heard that all baby animals are cute, which makes them less vulnerable to attack. Was that Your plan, Lord? I like to think so. I know how precious a newborn baby is, a reminder that You want the world to go on. What a relief, what a joy, to know You had the well-being of my children, of all children, in mind before they were even conceived. You wrote down the days of their lives before the foundation of the world. Keep me from hindering a child's love for You in any way. Use me to lead the little ones to You. Amen.

What Do You Want?
(MARK 10:46–52)

Lord Jesus, like Bartimaeus, I cry, "Jesus, have mercy on me!" Wonder of wonders, You stop. You call for me. And You don't offer a simple "God be with you." You ask me, "What do you want?" Like Bartimaeus, I want to see! More of You, more in Your Word, more of Your beauty. I want eyes to view other people as You do. I want Xray vision that uncovers the sin hidden deep in my heart, farsightedness that takes me forward in Your will. Lord, I want to see, that I may live as You have called me to. Amen.

Day 68

———⟨૭⟩૭——

NUMBERS 6:22–7:47
MARK 11
PSALM 49:10–20

Benediction

(NUMBERS 6:24–26)

Lord God, I offer the Aaronic blessing as a prayer for the people around me: The Lord bless you with plenty, in every circumstance, and with answered prayers. The Lord keep you, in safety, by His faithfulness that will never fail you. The Lord make His face shine upon you, that you may be aware of His glorious presence and respond in worship. The Lord be gracious to you, that you may live in that assurance and extend it to others. The Lord lift up His countenance upon you, revealing what few have seen, exposing sin, filling you with His light. The Lord give you peace in His presence, unlike what the world gives. Amen.

The Listening Ear
(Psalm 50:1–15)

Numbers 7:48–8:4
Mark 12:1–27
Psalm 50:1–15

Mighty God. The God who will not be silent. Perfect in beauty. God of justice. You are the God who is my God. You have commanded me to listen, for You want to speak uninterrupted. You don't need anything from me. You are entirely self-sufficient. You don't want offerings that are made without thanksgiving and obedience. You want me to call on You because I want You. It's all about relationship. You want me to call on You in trouble so that You may deliver me, so that I may give You thanks and honor. May I learn to live in that state of constant expectation and communication. Clean out my ears; teach me to listen more than speak. Amen.

The Widow's Offering
(MARK 12:41–44)

NUMBERS 8:5–9:23
MARK 12:28–44
PSALM 50:16–23

*L*ord Jesus, I lay myself before You, ashamed at how little I have given to You. You know my struggles with tithing. And yet, this woman gave everything she had to You. I've been a single mom, but I never gave away those last two pennies. Open my heart, open my hands, to give freely, sacrificially, with joy. You don't ask me to be financially irresponsible. But perhaps You do ask me to give until it's no longer easy or convenient. To give up something I want but don't need. Let me learn from You how to give, even if it means giving the most precious thing in my life. Amen.

Setting Out

NUMBERS 10–11
MARK 13:1–8
PSALM 51:1–9

*L*ord God, as I start this new day, I already know You are clearing the trail before me. I punch in, ready to go to work. Do as You promised. Chase my enemies away. Hold my head high so I can walk through their midst confidently and without fear. At day's end, when I come to rest, stay with me. Stand guard over my bed. I pray this not just for myself but for all Your people, the countless thousands across the globe. Let us not move unless You go with us and not stop until You give the signal. Amen.

Day 72

A Broken Spirit

(PSALM 51:10–19)

NUMBERS 12–13

MARK 13:9–37

PSALM 51:10–19

"Create in me a pure heart, O God" (Psalm 51:10 NIV). How many millions have repeated David's prayer? I bow before You in supplication. Oh Lord, forgive me for the times I've sinned! Oh Lord, transform me! I thank You for replacing my heart of stone with a new heart, in the sacrifice of Your Son and by the power of Your Spirit that raised Jesus from the dead. Break me, God, that I may see my sinfulness. Broken and contrite, desperate for a drop of Your mercy, I trust that You will draw near to me when at last I acknowledge I am unworthy to be in Your presence. Amen.

Olive Tree

(Psalm 52:8–9)

God, when I'm tempted to make fun of my enemies, may I instead watch them in holy fear, recognizing it could be me making wealth my god like they do, not You, my stronghold. Instead of being uprooted and thrown away, I'm that olive tree flourishing in Your garden. I trust in Your love because I can't outrun it or escape it. For all You have done, are doing, and will do for me, I praise You in the presence of others. I hope in Your name, for You are good. Amen!

Day 74

———⁂———

NUMBERS 15
MARK 14:32–72
PSALM 53

Troubled Prayer
(MARK 14:32–36)

*L*ord Jesus, how many times I've come to You feeling "deeply distressed"! And You understand what I'm going through, for You faced Your own prayer battle, overwhelmed with sorrow, to the point of death. My battles with depression, of feeling life isn't worth living, are only a pale reflection of Your sorrow when You sweat drops of blood and knew You were about to die and bear the sin of the world on Your shoulders. If Your heavenly Father would not spare You when You begged for any other way for humankind to be saved, who am I to complain about my trivial travails? In those dark times, may I look to this holy time and lean on You. Amen.

Election Times
(NUMBERS 16)

NUMBERS 16
MARK 15:1–32
PSALM 54

*L*ord, You know how fervently I have prayed during national elections. Sometimes the candidates I voted for won; sometimes they lost. I confess that when the president disappoints me, fulfilling my worst fears, I think, *God? God?* I question Your hand behind our country. Oh Lord, I'm like the people of Israel, talking against Your appointed leader. Tens of thousands of Americans prayed for the elections. Forgive me for second-guessing Your leadership. I rest in the knowledge that Your will for the president, for me personally, and for my country may not match my own vision for our future. Of course I want You to bless America. More than that, I pray that You will teach America to bless You. Amen.

Day 76

Watchful Women

(MARK 15:40–41)

NUMBERS 17–18

MARK 15:33–47

PSALM 55

*L*ord Jesus, I admit that the woman in me is proud of Mary Magdalene, Mary the mother of James, Salome, and all the other unnamed women who waited at the cross. Would I have had their courage, their stamina, to keep watch publicly? I thank You for their example. I thank You for the faithful service of church women through the years. But mostly I ask that my faith be like theirs—strong, able to endure the most painful test and to keep watch with those going through the hardest times. May I stand up for You even when it isn't popular, when it appears hopeless. Amen.

Meribah
(Numbers 20:12)

*H*eavenly Father, I can't imagine how Moses felt when You said he wouldn't enter the promised land. Of course, instead, he went to *the* promised land—the real Narnia, as C. S. Lewis put it—and how he must have rejoiced in that crossing over. But standing on this side of life's river, I don't quite understand the harshness of Your edict. I accept it by faith, and I pray I will learn from its lessons. And I pray for the times when I face disappointment, everything from losing mobility to having a book deal fall through. I thank You for allowing me to see into the future in the faces of my grandchildren. Amen.

Under Vows

(PSALM 56:8–13)

NUMBERS 21:1–22:20

LUKE 1:1–25

PSALM 56:8–13

I am under vows to You, my God, vows to bring an offering of thanksgiving before You. And I will thank You not because everything is going well and streams of abundance flow. Although I do give thanks for those times, now I give You thanks for the times that I stumble and You lift me up. That You give me life today. I offer myself as a living sacrifice. I can do nothing else. You are for me. Man can do nothing to me. I trust You and Your Word, and You take away my fear. Oh, give thanks to the Lord, for You are good! Amen.

The Magnificat
(LUKE 1:46–56)

NUM. 22:21–23:30
LUKE 1:26–56
PSALM 57

God my Savior, my soul glorifies You; I rejoice in You. Just as You were mindful of Mary, You are mindful of me. You saw me in my humble state and lifted me from the depths. Holy is Your name. May the news of Your mighty deeds on my behalf be told to future generations. May the great- and great-great-grandchildren who won't meet me hear of the God I served. Your mercy extends to me and to a thousand generations. You showed mercy to Mary through her cousin Elizabeth. I thank You for the grace bearers and grace givers in my life. Amen!

Changing Winds
(Numbers 24)

NUMBERS 24–25
LUKE 1:57–2:20
PSALM 58

*D*ear Lord, I confess I'm uncomfortable with this aspect of prayer, that the prayer You place on my heart isn't the one I expect or want. Like when You want me to bless my enemies instead of cursing them. Of course You wanted to bless Israel, but later You sent Jonah to Nineveh, demanding he bless his enemy by sharing Your word with them. Lord, praying for my enemies is like a wrestling match. Bring my spirit into alignment with Your will. Once You have shown me that will, may I act promptly—even if it means blessing my enemy. I ask especially that You break down any hostility between me and others. Amen.

Adapting

(NUMBERS 27:1–11)

NUMBERS 26:1–27:11
LUKE 2:21–38
PSALM 59:1–8

*L*ord God, how thankful I am that You won't leave me as a second-class citizen without rights any more than You did Zelophehad's daughters. I throw myself on Your mercy, grateful You didn't set me aside because I grew up in a single-parent home or when my marriage failed. You saw *me*, a person created by You and in Your image, and You made me a coheir with Your Son. I pray that I will live as a princess in Your kingdom, endued with Your beauty, clothed in Your salvation, carrying out kingdom duties. Amen.

Day 82

When I Die

(Numbers 27:15–21)

Numbers 27:12–29:11

Luke 2:39–52

Psalm 59:9–17

Heavenly Father, how I hope that the prayers I offer when I die are as focused on others as Moses' were, as my mother's were. Mold me in the fashion of elder saints over the centuries. Moses asked for someone to lead Israel, and You appointed Joshua. I pray for my family, as my son and then his children pick up the mantle of spiritual leadership. That Your light will burn as brightly in all four grandchildren down to the youngest as it does in their father. I pray for my church community, my fellow writers, my friends—that You will bring someone to fill the voids I may leave behind. Then take me home. I'm ready. Amen.

While Jesus Was Praying

(LUKE 3:21–22)

Day 83

NUMBERS 29:12–30:16
LUKE 3
PSALM 60:1–5

*L*ord Jesus, what did You say on the day of Your baptism? You didn't have any sins to confess. Were You celebrating? Asking for Your Father's blessing and strength as You began a public ministry, fully revealing Yourself as Messiah? Thanking God for Your cousin and praying for him? I thank You that You allowed us to see and hear part of that prayer, when the Father spoke for human ears to hear and the Holy Spirit came on You like a dove for all to see. I pray that my time with You will make me transparent, that others can see You in me. Amen.

Day 84

NUMBERS 31
LUKE 4
PSALM 60:6–12

You Are Mine

(PSALM 60:6–12)

*O*h Lord whose name is Holy, how I love this passage, the possessive note in Your voice. "Gilead is mine, and Manasseh is mine; Ephraim is my helmet, Judah is my scepter" (Psalm 60:7 NIV). I hear the echoes. "Darlene is mine!" Before I ask, You are shouting triumph over my enemies, even when they come from my own family. So with confidence I approach You, asking for Your aid. Convict me when I seek human help for something only You can provide. With You I will gain the victory. Not by myself alone, but with all others who belong to You. Amen.

Lead Me to the Rock

(PSALM 61:2–4)

NUMBERS 32–33
LUKE 5:1–16
PSALM 61

*H*ear my cry, oh Lord; listen to my prayer. When I am under pressure, my heart overwhelmed, when joy and peace are being squeezed out of it, lead me to the rock that is higher than I. Place me where the enemy cannot reach me. You have been my shelter and a strong tower in the past. You will be yet again. I will dwell in Your tabernacle, shielded by Your glory and holiness. In Your presence, clothed in Your righteousness and salvation, I will shine brightly before all who oppose me. I rest as a baby chick under the shelter of those powerful wings. Amen.

Day 86

Numbers 34–36
Luke 5:17–32
Psalm 62:1–6

You Are My Rock
(Psalm 62)

Heavenly Father, when I cannot sleep, when I am consumed by worry, let me run to You and cuddle in Your loving arms. My hope comes from You. I will arise with renewed encouragement for the day ahead. You are my rock. You make me strong, unbreakable when I take my stand on You. You are my salvation. You renew my spirit. You are my fortress. I walk in the force field of Your love, protected from harm. Let me take rest on a regular basis, that I will rise with wings like eagles. Amen.

Do It My Way

DEUT. 1:1–2:25
LUKE 5:33–6:11
PSALM 62:7–12

*L*iving Word, imprint on my heart the principle You gave to the Pharisees: "Which is lawful: to save life or destroy it?" I confess that I sometimes create destruction by being stuck in my way of doing things, that I take away someone else's joy by standing up for my rights. Forgive me, Lord. You have come to free me from rigidity in my thoughts and spirit and life. There is only one way to salvation, but I sometimes get discouraged by theological discord. Let me follow the leading of Your Spirit, informed by Your written Word. Amen.

Slake My Thirst
(PSALM 63:1–5)

DEUT. 2:26–4:14

LUKE 6:12–35

PSALM 63:1–5

God, You are my God. I seek You, thirsting, panting, coughing, unable to swallow or breathe without You. I stumble through the desert where I find myself and remember the days of glory when I saw You in Your sanctuary. In the desert, Your power and glory seem like a mirage. But by faith I cling to them. Your love is better than life. You give me a reason to live. I choose to glorify You with my lips, to praise You today and every day, to lift up my hands in Your name, to sing to You. I know that You will satisfy that hunger and slake that thirst with the best of the land. Amen.

Bring Me Back

(DEUTERONOMY 4:29–31)

Heavenly Lord, You are not just God; You are my God, and You always treat me with compassion. What I may perceive as ruin is only Your way of guiding me back to renewing my vows. You are my God, always faithful to me, never breaking Your covenant with me even when I've given You grounds. Whatever ruins I perceive in my life are Your gifts, meant to guide me back to the center of Your will. God who fashioned every moment of my life, teach me to follow with ever more of my heart and soul, until I give You my all. Amen.

Day 90

The Lonely Widow

(LUKE 7:11–17)

DEUT. 5:23–7:26

LUKE 7:1–17

PSALM 64:1–5

*L*ord Jesus, how I rejoice because I love You and trust You with all my being. Like the woman in today's passage, I lost my husband, my daughter too, and it seemed I was about to lose my son. But You called him back from the edge of destruction and despair and gave him back to me alive. How I thank You and rejoice in You. I thank You for the gift of my family. I praise You that I can rest, that I can trust You in life and in death. Amen.

Clothes That Don't Wear Out
(Deuteronomy 8:4)

Deuteronomy 8–9
Luke 7:18–35
Psalm 64:6–10

*L*ord, how I thank You for the heavenly uniform You have given me. Every day I commune with You, it shines more brightly than the day before. It will never wear out. In my emperor's new clothes, I fade away while You shine ever more brightly in me. From the helmet of salvation on my head to shoes made from the sturdy, soft leather of the Gospel of peace on my feet and the garment of Your righteousness, Your holiness, covering my body, I couldn't ask for better clothing. You have given me forever-wear, all that I need for today and throughout eternity. God—the best couture ever. Thank You, Lord. Amen.

Day 92

Deut. 10–11
Luke 7:36–8:3
Psalm 65:1–8

Worshipping with Prisoners
(Luke 7:36–43)

Loving Lord, I confess I'm more like the Pharisees than the sinful woman in this story. I smell someone with the spiritual odor of sin clinging to them when they come to worship and I judge. Forgive me, Lord! In You there is no male or female, no slave or free—no prisoner or prison guard. Lord, if anything, I ask that You will bring more "sinners" into my life. May I learn from their humility, from their outpouring of love because You have forgiven what I consider the unforgiveable. Break my spirit so that I may accept them as my equals, brothers and sisters in Christ. Amen.

Testing

Lord God, I wonder if I'd be any more prepared for Your tests if I knew about them ahead of time? Instead they show up when least expected, like pop quizzes. I pray that I won't listen to people who offer to help me cheat, that I won't be led astray by false signs and wonders or believe anyone who speaks of a false god. Fan the flames of love in my heart, so that passion for You may burn brightly deep within. May its kindling fuel my obedience, light my service, and provide the adhesive that keeps me fast to You. Amen.

Drowning
(LUKE 8:22–25)

DEUT. 14:1–16:8

LUKE 8:22–39

PSALM 66:1–7

*M*aster, I'm going to drown! How many times has my cry echoed that of the disciples? How often I've seen the leaping waves and tried to bail out my sinking boat. I know You're there, but sometimes it seems like You're asleep, not paying any attention. Forgive me for trying to solve the problem by myself. Forgive me for my lack of faith, for not coming to You before the situation reached a crisis stage. Oh Lord, how I thank You that You are in the boat with me when the storm is raging. The next time I'm about to capsize, may I turn to You, asking You to speak, "Peace, be still," to my heart. Amen.

Faith vs. Fear

(LUKE 8:50)

DEUT. 16:9–18:22
LUKE 8:40–56
PSALM 66:8–15

Heavenly Father, I come before You this morning, a heart in despair. My beloved child is dead, and I feel as though my heart has been torn in two. I confess I am listening to inner condemnation that says if I had been a better mother, she wouldn't have died. Oh Lord, forgive me for wrong thinking. Create in me a new mind. You tell me not to be afraid. You command me to turn the loss over to You and to believe in You, not what You will do. When my feet are planted in You, I will sing praises to You, free from fear. Nothing I might lose can compare to what I gain in You. Amen.

Day 96

Deut. 19:1–21:9
Luke 9:1–22
Psalm 66:16–20

A Time to Stay Home
(Deuteronomy 20:5–9)

Compassionate God, how I thank You for these instructions to Moses. You don't call me to a life of constant battle. Your plan tells me to invest time in my family and to take care of what You've given me. I confess I struggle with finding the right balance. At times I shut myself off from others. Other times I keep so busy with activities that I neglect what's important. I pray that Your loving wisdom will guide me as I schedule my days. Show me when to say no. Teach me to handle the unexpected with grace. Amen.

Make Me a Blessing
(Psalm 67:1–2)

Deut. 21:10–23:8
Luke 9:23–42
Psalm 67

*G*racious God, how often have I prayed the first half of this prayer, that You will bless me and cause Your face to shine on me. I praise You for the beauty of the second half of the prayer. When You bless me, make Your ways known upon the earth, Your salvation among all nations. I ask the same for all believers, that Your blessing may be so obvious that others might clamor for the way for themselves, that a single candle will become two then three until whole villages and regions blaze with Your fullness and light. Amen.

Counting the Cost

(LUKE 9:57–62)

DEUT. 23:9–25:19

LUKE 9:43–62

PSALM 68:1–6

*L*ord, even my dull human spirit can see the contra-
diction between calling You "Lord" but saying "wait
a minute" before I obey. Your standards haven't changed.
You'll ask me to let go of whatever I most want to put
in Your place. You're a jealous God, and You won't share Your glory with another. I
confess, I don't always understand how that works. But do I value Your good gifts
more than You, the Giver? May it never be. May I not look to the side, at what others
are doing. May I not look back, at what might have been. Instead, may I turn my
gaze upon You, the author and finisher of my faith. Amen.

Inspection Time

*L*ord God, everything I am and have belongs to You, but within that framework You've given me money to take care of my needs. Thank You for that gift, that trust. Teach me the discipline of setting aside some of those funds, and my time, to give to others who are in need. Make me a living sacrifice of worship. Oh Lord, how I long to say with confidence that I've obeyed *all* Your commands, for that is what You require. You desire more than my offering. You want my obedience. Forgive me when I fail at either. Amen.

Thinking like a Child
(LUKE 10:21)

DEUT. 28:15–68

LUKE 10:21–37

PSALM 68:15–19

*L*ord Jesus, make my prayer like Yours. Fill me with Your joy through the Holy Spirit, that I may return praise to Your Father. Joyful, full of praise, I fall in wonder before You, the Lord of heaven and earth. *You* are the Lord, not the wise or rich or powerful of the earth. May I approach You like a child expecting good gifts from my Father. Lord, forgive me if I come like a know-it-all, thinking I only need to ask Your opinion to compare to mine. May I accept Your ways as best without question. You want to bless Your children. How I wonder and rejoice in that. Amen.

Learning the Lesson

(DEUTERONOMY 29:2–6)

DEUT. 29–30
LUKE 10:38–11:23
PSALM 68:20–27

Lord, I laugh at Israel for their failure to learn lessons after forty years. But You're reminding me, *"What about the things I've been teaching you during your sixty-plus years?"* Oh Lord, forgive me for ever taking You for granted! As I go about my day, bring to mind the things You've done in my lifetime. Instruct my inner being through what You've done for Your people in the past. May I give thanks for everything as Your gracious provision, instead of treating it as my right. Through it all, open my eyes to see that You are God. You are *my* God. Amen.

Day 102

God on Display
(PSALM 68:28–35)

DEUT. 31:1–32:22
LUKE 11:24–36
PSALM 68:28–35

$\mathcal{G}$od of the nations, display Your awesome power. Fill the earth with the sound of Your mighty thunder summoning Your strength. I pray that the people of the earth will bring tribute to You, acknowledging Your lordship over them as individuals and nations. Make "in God we trust" more than words on our money. I pray for the people of the earth, especially those who don't know You, that they will submit themselves to You. That they'll sing to You and proclaim Your power. May they fall in worship and accept Your offer of salvation. Amen.

Save Me, Lord
(Psalm 69:1–9)

Save me, oh God, I cry one more time. Lord, I'm weary of calling for help. I'm floundering. My feet can't find a foothold. Your Spirit must carry my prayers, for my voice is gone. My eyes have failed; I no longer see You. Everything has been stripped from me, and people are demanding I pay for things I never took. Deliver me from the depths I've plunged into out of my own choice. Forgive me both for my own sin and especially for the disgrace I have brought upon people who hope in You. I come to You because You've always been my help before. Amen.

Day 104

Joshua's Call
(JOSHUA 1:1–9)

DEUT. 34–JOSHUA 2
LUKE 12:1–15
PSALM 69:10–17

Wow, God, what a difference between Joshua and Moses. Moses kept asking You to send someone else, but Joshua went right to work. Make me more like Joshua than like Moses—at least when it comes to what You've called me to do. I'm very thankful You haven't commissioned me to lead an army bent on conquering. But whether I'm a five-star general or a stay-at-home mom, bend my will to obey. *"Don't be afraid. I'm with you wherever you go."* I praise You for the promise. Reveal Your will for this day, as You did for Joshua. Amen.

Treasure That Won't Corrupt
(LUKE 12:32–34)

JOSHUA 3:1–5:12
LUKE 12:16–40
PSALM 69:18–28

*L*ord of heaven, You've entrusted Your kingdom to me. I tremble at that confidence. Today and every day, may I exchange the treasures of my sharecrop farm for the glory of Your kingdom. Teach me to invest, not in silver and gold, but in the coin of Your realm, which will never be taken away. I'm not sure what the treasure I'm accumulating consists of. A desire to know You? People I've influenced for good? Praise to You? Whatever it is, it's of infinite value. Let me live each day with eternal values in view. Amen.

When You Fall

(JOSHUA 7:1–12)

JOSHUA 5:13–7:26

LUKE 12:41–48

PSALM 69:29–36

*O*h Lord, how I know Joshua's feelings after Ai. Just when everything seems to be going well, I rely on myself or hold back something that belongs to You and down I go. Forgive me for using my words to build myself up. Take them, take me, and use me to glorify Your name. Correct my steps so that I follow Your commands, not in selfish pursuits. Forgive me, Lord, when I grab ahold of something that belongs to You and bury it deep, saving it for myself. Forgive me for the harm I bring to my children. Amen.

Judging for Myself
(LUKE 12:57)

Lord, I confess I doubt myself and Your calling far beyond what is reasonable. Not that doubt is reasonable since You're the all-powerful God, but You welcome honest questions. Do spiritual giants struggle with doubt? Did Billy Graham ever question if he had anything worthwhile to share when he preached? Did C. S. Lewis wonder if his books would help anyone? Remind me that any good that comes from my actions, my words, flows from You. It's not whether I'm prepared but whether I trust You to do what You've promised. Whenever I'm questioning You, counsel me to accept Your judgment. Show me when it's a good time to ask for advice and when to trust You without question. Amen.

Day 108

Hope Endures

(PSALM 71:1–6)

JOSHUA 10:1–11:15

LUKE 13:1–21

PSALM 71:1–6

*L*ord God, You've been my hope since my youth. Oh, how my soul rejoices in that confidence. Thank You for saving me at a young age and for leading me. Your sovereign will redirected me when I pursued a false lead. I thank You for the strength that hope gave me with each twist and turn. And I rejoice in hope, because of joy. Completion and new beginnings await me when I follow You. Forgive me for the times I let the embers burn low and I allowed myself to wallow in despair. What can I add to Your perfect foresight? Nothing. I rest in that hope. Amen.

Hope Today and Always
(PSALM 71:7–16)

JOSHUA 11:16–13:33
LUKE 13:22–35
PSALM 71:7–16

*M*y Living Hope, I'll always have hope. It's based on Your character and Your faithfulness. In my short memory, You have never failed me—or anyone who has trusted You. The more I praise You, the more my expectation increases. When I speak today, let me speak of Your righteous deeds, Your saving acts. Fill my mouth with news of Your saving acts—I'll never run out of stories to share. Let me proclaim Your mighty works, and not those of mortal man. As I teach my family, let me lift You up as our Standard. Amen.

Give Me This Mountain

(Joshua 14:6–15)

JOSHUA 14–16
LUKE 14:1–15
PSALM 71:17–21

*H*eavenly Father, like Caleb, I'm drawing near the end of my life. I'm checking in: What about those dreams and visions You gave me that haven't been fulfilled? I celebrate the mountains You've put me on that I didn't ask for. But I want that mountain before I die. You know my frailty. Unlike Caleb, my vigor isn't what it once was. Clear my vision, increase the acuteness of my mind, give me strength for the day—equip me for the battle for what is yet to be. May all glory be returned to You. Amen.

JOSHUA 17:1–19:16
LUKE 14:16–35
PSALM 71:22–24

*Y*ou say I can't be Your disciple if I don't pick up my cross. Do I dare ask—but what is that cross? It's not wood I can buy at a lumberyard or something I wear around my neck. Do You give one to every Christian, along with a new heart? Or is it tailor-made for me? You ask me to pay a price for my cross. It might be letting go of my family or letting go of my life. Following You comes with a price tag, and that scares me. When decision time comes, will I hold back when You demand every penny in my life's wallet? Stamp out my fear of future sacrifice by giving me strength for today. Amen.

Day 112

Sanctuary

(JOSHUA 20)

JOSHUA 19:17–21:42

LUKE 15:1–10

PSALM 72:1–11

*L*ord of lords, what a wonder that the God who runs the universe considers the needs of the falsely accused. You arranged for them to have a safe place to await trial. But over the years, we've stretched the concept of Your provision and perhaps even misapplied it. I pray for my country, that its government, its cities and people will align themselves with Your Word in providing places of refuge. I pray for wisdom in handling refugees and prisoners. For the justice system. I pray that You will provide sanctuary for political and persecuted refugees. Reveal to us what that looks like in the twenty-first century. Amen.

The Prodigal Son
(Luke 15:11–32)

Joshua 21:43–22:34
Luke 15:11–32
Psalm 72:12–20

Heavenly Father, in the parable of the prodigal son, I'm the angry older brother, aren't I? You know the struggles I had growing up as an only child, when Mom seemed to favor her step-grandchildren. Remove that big ball of feeling entitled and ignored. Correct me, that I may switch the attitude of complaining to one of gratitude. Open my eyes to Your constant love that never changes. I thank You that when I was that prodigal, seeking a way home, You ran to greet me and dressed me in Your new clothes. I thank You for the older brothers and sisters who welcomed me to the family. Amen.

Day 114

JOSHUA 23–24
LUKE 16:1–18
PSALM 73:1–9

Choices

(JOSHUA 24)

Lord God, the challenge Joshua issued at the end of his life rings deep in my heart, cutting and convicting me. I thank You for the people who came before me who said, "We will serve the Lord." I thank You for those who stand with me, that together we affirm, "We will serve the Lord!" I rejoice in my children holding place with our family, repeating the oath. Make that choice real in the give-and-take of my daily life, that I will do as I've promised. You know the truth, that what I promise today I will struggle to fulfill tomorrow and ten years from now. Keep my heart steadfast on You. Amen.

Testing Stones
(Judges 2:1–3)

Judges 1–2
Luke 16:19–17:10
Psalm 73:10–20

*L*ord of hosts, this passage terrifies me. I love hearing the sweet, gentle voice of Your Wonderful Counselor. I freeze in the presence of Your angel and the pronouncement of guilt and punishment. I confess, I've messed up; I've broken the covenant I made when my children were small. Oh Lord, how am I to contend with the high places I didn't break down in the strength of my youth? You leave them there to test me and, even worse, to test my descendants. Oh Lord, forgive me! Please spare them. In Your strength, those ingrained behaviors can be demolished. Amen.

Day 116

The Thankful Leper

(LUKE 17:11–17)

JUDGES 3–4

LUKE 17:11–37

PSALM 73:21–28

Jesus, Master and Savior, have pity on me! I'm broken and discarded, spurned by other discards of society. Before I could know what You were about, while I was on my way, You spoke and made me whole. Oh, I never thought I could ever be free of the sin disease, and yet You restored what the foxes have eaten. Let me always be like the one leper who came back to thank You. Too often I take Your gifts for granted. Thank You that You take that tiniest sliver of faith—which You gave to me—and grow it into this miracle! Amen.

Patience in Prayer
(LUKE 18:1–8)

Heavenly Father, what a thought. Do you teach me about delayed satisfaction in my life, that I will know better how to persist in prayer? Sometimes I pray and the answer comes, quickly and clearly. More often, I lift up a concern and wonder why the answer doesn't come. But then it does, in the blink of an eye, in such a way that only You could have done it. Wow, that's it, isn't it? When the answer comes that way, all the glory goes only to You. Oh Lord, may You find me faithful. Amen.

Day 118

Gideon's Fleece
(JUDGES 6:36–40)

JUDGES 6:25–7:25
LUKE 18:18–43
PSALM 74:4–11

Lord God, how I thank You for Your patience with Gideon. I thank You for this example. When You call me to do something that's unexpected and unlikely, if not impossible, I rest, knowing I can ask for confirmation. I pray I will imitate Gideon's faith, that I will demolish idols and magnify Your name. I don't need confirmation to know that's Your will. But when I'm asking You to move the mountains that stand between me and what I believe You want me to do, I want to be sure about what I'm doing. Thank You for the fleeces that either blaze an open road or turn me aside from false trails. Amen.

Asaph's King

(PSALM 74:12–17)

God my King, You have placed people in authority over my country. But in all the years of my life, You are my only King. You, and You alone, have the right to be sovereign. Forgive me when I create minigods—myself, my family, my work. Knock them down, by whatever means, that You might reign in me. You are not only my Sovereign; You are also ruler of the earth. You are not only my Redeemer; You are also the Savior of the world. I long for the day when all people on earth worship You as Lord of lords. Amen.

Day 120

Poor and Needy
(PSALM 74:18–23)

JUDGES 9:22–10:18

LUKE 19:29–48

PSALM 74:18–23

Sovereign Lord, may the poor and needy praise Your name. When I was poverty-stricken and without resources, You answered my prayer. I intercede for those without any form of support. For those who are as defenseless as turtledoves—rescue them. For those who are suffering in spirit, body, or mind—heal them. For those who have been humiliated—remember them. Lift them up. Make the lame walk and the blind see. Free the prisoners. Comfort those who are grieving. Above all, may You satisfy their hunger for righteousness and save them from the depths of sin. How I praise You for all You have done and will do. Amen.

Cornerstone

(LUKE 20:17–18)

JUDGES 11:1–12:7
LUKE 20:1–26
PSALM 75:1–7

*J*esus, You are the cornerstone. I stand on You; I hide in the cleft of Your rock when evil lurks. Your granite surface is the measuring stick for my beliefs and practices. I trust in You, depend on You, and praise You. Woe be to me if I ever stop trusting in You. The rock will become a millstone around my neck, pulling me under. It will break my bones and my spirit when I land on it like a free-fall skydive. It will grind me to fine powder and use my life's wheat. How I thank You that, even then, You can take those broken pieces and make me whole again. Amen.

The Living and the Dead
(LUKE 20:34–38)

JUDGES 12:8–14:20
LUKE 20:27–47
PSALM 75:8–10

*L*iving God, how final death looms to those of us still living on this earth. We miss our loved ones fiercely. The death of strangers—whether by illness or violence or neglect—troubles us. Too soon, we cry. How I take comfort in these verses. You are the God of the living! Everyone who belongs to You lives forever with You. Oh Lord, say hi to my grandmother, my mother, my daughter, all with You. Teach me to live the life You have given here and now to the full. I trust You that my ever-after will be more glorious and wonderful than anything I have ever known. I join with the living, in heaven and on earth, in praising Your name. Amen.

Samson's Two Prayers
(Judges 15:18, 16:18)

Day 123

JUDGES 15–16
LUKE 21:1–19
PSALM 76:1–7

*W*hat a difference between Samson's two prayers, Lord. I confess that my prayers are often like that of the young Samson, arrogant, selfish, shortsighted. Was there a kernel of faith in bringing those requests to You, the Great Giver? And not seeking help elsewhere? May my spirit become more like that of the older Samson. When my life is in tatters, make me humble and penitent, with a sacrificial spirit. Remember me, Lord, not because I'm anyone special, but for Your sake. Restore the strength of my youth one last time, that Your name will be known far and wide and You will be glorified. Amen.

Everlasting Words
(LUKE 21:33)

JUDGES 17–18

LUKE 21:20–22:6

PSALM 76:8–12

First You deliver the bad news—heaven and earth, the universe as I know it, will come to an end. The matter You've created will disappear, and that's scary. But then You give the good news—Your words won't pass away. When I am left alone, in the void, Your words—You Yourself!—are there. They last forever, never disappearing. Nothing can destroy them. They are forever true, never wearing out, always up-to-date. They will always accomplish Your purpose. Oh Lord, may I meditate on Your Word, memorize it, feast on it, for then I shall be eternally satisfied. Amen.

Who's Listening?
(PSALM 77:1–11)

Lord God, like Jeduthun, I cry out to You. My spirit shouts. I thank You that it's okay to cry for You when I'm in distress. Sometimes I wonder if You're listening. But Your Spirit is convicting me, asking me, *"Which is more important: for God to listen to you—or for you to listen to God?"* Forgive me for thinking prayer is all about me! Clear the clouds of doubt and fear from my vision, the echoes of despair from my hearing, that I may see and hear You. Perhaps the darkness has come to teach me to truly listen. Amen.

Day 126

JUDGES 20:24–21:25

LUKE 22:31–54

PSALM 77:12–20

Enter Not into Temptation
(LUKE 22:39–46)

*L*ord Jesus, bend my heart to obey Your words. I pray that I'll not enter into temptation when I'm feeling pressure because of new problems or everyday stress. May I put on my full armor, from the helmet of salvation to the Gospel-of-peace shoes to the sword of the Spirit. Teach me the discipline of prayer to prepare for battle. I'm absolutely blown away that You wanted Your disciples to pray for their needs when You were facing death. How often do I stand on the edge of an unseen precipice and fail to follow Your preparation instructions? Forgive me. Yet in Your grace You rescue me. Amen.

Ruth's Prayer

RUTH 1–2
LUKE 22:55–23:25
PSALM 78:1–4

*L*ord God, how I thank You for the women of the Bible, for their real problems and their astonishing acts of faith. But among them all, Ruth is one of my favorites. How I praise You for the testimony coming from a woman who wasn't from Israel. May You deal with me if I fail in fidelity to those I owe my love, service, and support. When You lead me into strange lands, may I move forward boldly, gleaning in the fields if that's the only work I can find. Open my eyes to the helping community, like Boaz and his fields, that You have prepared for me in that new place. Grant me the humility to accept the task, no matter how humble. Amen.

Day 128

Dying Prayers
(LUKE 23:32–46)

RUTH 3–4
LUKE 23:26–24:12
PSALM 78:5–8

Lord Jesus, Your final words make me uncomfortable because death seems so final and the passage difficult. I pray that when my time approaches, I will reflect the same grace and priorities as You did. That stops me. I pray to my living Savior because You died and yet now You live. There's my hope. You prayed for forgiveness for those who killed You. May I also seek reconciliation with those who have wronged me—whom I have wronged—before I die. You also continued Your mission of bringing people into the kingdom. May I continue to share the good news with my last breath. Let me commit myself as fully to You in death as I have in life. Amen.

Hannah's Prayer

(1 Samuel 1)

1 Samuel 1:1–2:21
Luke 24:13–53
Psalm 78:9–16

Dear Lord, how many parents have followed Hannah's example in giving their children back to You? I did. My precious daughter was a special gift from You, and she knew she was an answer to prayer. I thank You for that testimony, but I also remember the pain that came with it. The fear of losing her in the womb prompted the first prayer, and pain ripped me in half when she died too young. I pray for all those who are childless, for those whose children have died. Comfort our grief. Fill our empty arms with Your fullness and joy. Our disappointment will lead to Your best for us. Let us cling to that in faith. Amen.

Day 130

You Came to Your Own

(JOHN 1:9–13)

1 SAMUEL 2:22–4:22

JOHN 1:1–28

PSALM 78:17–24

*L*ord Jesus, when I received You, You also received me. Joy sings in my soul because it's a mutual relationship. You adopted me and gave me legal rights entitling me to everything You have. You did more than take me into Your family. You rebirthed me, re-creating my soul and spirit. I am Your child because I am made new in Your likeness. Your paternity now defines me. Miracle of miracles, You softened my heart to believe in You. Oh Lord, I pray for those who still refuse to accept Your gift of salvation. Convict them; bring them back to You. Amen.

In Spite of It All
(PSALM 78:25–33)

1 SAMUEL 5–7
JOHN 1:29–51
PSALM 78:25–33

*L*ord God, when I read these verses, I want to hide under a rock. I confess I'm like the Israelites. I gorge on all Your good gifts until I'm sick, and then I blame You because I'm not doing well. When You correct me, too often I ignore Your conviction and keep on sinning. Can't I see the direction I'm headed in? If I don't pay attention and change my ways, the gifts may stop. I wind up unsatisfied, in utter futility—in terror, in fact. For once I have known Your goodness, Your absence is frightening. Do whatever it takes to bring me to my senses. Bring me to repentance before it's too late. Amen.

Day 132

Only Flesh

(PSALM 78:34–41)

1 SAMUEL 8:1–9:26

JOHN 2

PSALM 78:34–41

L ord God, living for You is a continual act of faith. It goes against my instinct. I rub against a hard time and stumble and fall. Oh, forgive me when my doubt entices me to test You. Who do I think I am—a mere human, daring to bring a case against God? How rich is Your mercy to me, that You remember I am only flesh, a passing breeze that doesn't return. How great Your mercy, how expansive Your forgiveness. You are my Rock. You are my Redeemer. You will not allow me to wander too far away from You. I thank You for Your loving discipline that brings me back to You. Amen.

Shortsighted
(JOHN 3:1–22)

1 SAMUEL 9:27–11:15
JOHN 3:1–22
PSALM 78:42–55

ord Jesus, I like how Nicodemus acted on what he knew, that You were a teacher, a man sent from God to do miraculous deeds. If only more people would act on what little they know of You. He wanted to hear but didn't understand. If this man, a lifelong student of Your Word, misunderstood You so, what hope is there for me? I come to You, shortsighted and blind, and You offer me a second birth. Oh Lord, how I rejoice that I gain new eyes to see the wonderful things of Your Word, ears to hear Your voice, a heart to beat in time with Yours. Amen.

Far Be It from Me
(1 Samuel 12:20–25)

1 Samuel 12–13
John 3:23–4:10
Psalm 78:56–66

Lord God, make Samuel's promise my own. Far be it from me that I should sin against You by failing to pray for the people You've placed in my circle. Forgive me for my lapses in that area. Samuel made praying for Israel his life's work. I do pray for others—kind of. I phrase my thoughts of them as prayers. I hear their needs and my heart sends up a cry. I clasp their hands and pray right then and there. But do I follow through, pray until I know the answer? Ah, Lord. There is so much I still need to learn. Make me an instrument of prayer. Amen.

Rejecting Joseph
(PSALM 78:67–68)

Lord God, did I read that right? You *rejected* the tents of Joseph? Sure, You chose Judah, David's tribe, the Messiah's tribe. But I've never thought of it as actively rejecting Joseph. Why Judah and not godly Joseph? Joseph never slept with his dead son's widow. He never strayed from You that we know of. In the end Judah changed, offering himself in place of Benjamin. I take comfort that Joseph was a vital part of Israel, just not its designated leader. Ultimately, it's all about Your sovereignty. Jacob You loved; Esau You hated. Wonder of wonders: You chose me. Amen.

Day 136

Appearances

(1 SAMUEL 16:6–7)

1 SAMUEL 15–16

JOHN 4:39–54

PSALM 79:1–7

*L*ord, this morning, I worried about fixing my hair for a picture. Did any of Jesse's sons primp before they appeared before Samuel? The prophet showed his feet of clay here, looking at the striking appearance of Jesse's oldest son. Thanks for the reminder that I don't have to be perfect to follow You. But Samuel waited for Your leading as the father paraded healthy son after healthy son, all six of them, until only the youngest was left. Lord, when You bring someone into my life, forgive me if I reject them because of their appearance. May I train my eyes to see the true person beneath the externals. Amen.

The Battle Is the Lord's
(1 SAMUEL 17)

1 Samuel 17
John 5:1–24
Psalm 79:8–13

Lord God, I've faced some scary enemies, but I've never fought someone as physically imposing as Goliath. It would be like trying to stop a nuclear attack armed with only muskets. Did David's youth help him to have that single-minded confidence? Oh, to have that vision. Forgive me when I allow spears and javelins to eclipse the complete sovereign power of Your name. When Your enemies defy You, may I take up the battle. It belongs to You, and You will give the victory, whatever the weapons of my battlefield. In fact, I rejoice in my poor weapons because they show that You have saved, and You alone. Amen.

Day 138

Joseph's Shepherd
(PSALM 80:1–7)

1 SAMUEL 18–19

JOHN 5:25–47

PSALM 80:1–7

Oh Lord my God, You are not only the Shepherd of Israel. You are also the Shepherd of Joseph, Ephraim, Benjamin, Manasseh, and more. You are my Shepherd. You added me to Your flock. You called me by name. I heard Your voice and joined the others in Your sheep pen. Together, we bleat for Your protection. You are enthroned between the cherubim. Your light leads us. Lift up Your hands and save us. When we have wandered astray, restore us. Make Your face shine upon us, that we might be saved. That we might reflect Your glory, our new hearts as white as carded wool. Amen.

Friendship

1 Samuel 20–21
John 6:1–21
Psalm 80:8–19

*D*ear Lord, how I love to read about David and Jonathan. What a king Jonathan might have made. What sacrifice, love, and friendship he offered to David, knowing his best friend would take his place as Israel's next ruler. Oh Lord, when I see someone overtaking me, let me accept them with the same grace. How I grieved at the loss of my first writing friends and missed their support. Yet now You have replaced them with so many others. Thank You, Lord. If we must part ways, let us celebrate the bond You have created between us. I pray that You will go with them and give them success on their journey. Amen.

Day 140

---

1 SAMUEL 22–23
JOHN 6:22–42
PSALM 81:1–10

Bread of Life

(JOHN 6:30–40)

*B*read of Life, fill me, satisfy me. I ate of Your sacrifice and was born anew. Words can't express my gratitude, my deep joy, my soul-deep rest in that salvation. You are my Father, my all in all, and nothing can separate me from You. Now that I have tasted and seen that the Lord is good, I want more, so much more! May I open every crevice of my being for Your Spirit to fill and use me. I hunger for Your righteousness to mark me as Yours. I want a storehouse of Your goodness to give to others. Give me only what I need for today. I thank You that it will be all that I need. Amen.

To Whom Shall We Go?
(JOHN 6:67–71)

1 SAMUEL 24:1–25:31
JOHN 6:43–71
PSALM 81:11–16

*L*ord Jesus, I marvel at the close friendship between You and the disciples. How very human You sounded when You asked, "Are you going to leave Me too?" With Peter, I affirm, "Where else would I go? You alone have the words of life." I have come to believe because of Your gift of grace and faith. It's all from You. Peter saw You were the Messiah, God Himself, the Holy One of Israel. The more time I spend with You, the more I learn. The more I know of You, the more I want to spend time with You. I yearn for eternity with You, when we will speak face-to-face. Amen.

Day 142

David and Saul

(1 Samuel 26)

1 Samuel 25:32–27:12

John 7:1–24

Psalm 82

Sovereign Lord, how I thank You that no one is pursuing my life like Saul hunted David. May I have the grace to spare anyone who persecutes me, as David did Saul. I'm tempted to think You've delivered my enemy into my hands so I can act as judge and jury. Open my eyes, that I may see that person as You do. You love him. You want to bring him into the kingdom. You may even have special plans for him. Keep me from doing harm. Lead me in acts of reconciliation, and not retaliation. Amen.

....

....

....

....

....

....

....

....

....

....

....

....

....

....

Restoration

1 SAMUEL 28–29

JOHN 7:25–8:11

PSALM 83

Lord Jesus, whatever the textual uncertainty, I love what I learn about You from this story. It's so You. You show Yourself as the author of the wisdom that gave Solomon his reputation. You leveled the playing field. You removed the woman's accusers, their guilt clear, but Your concern was for the woman. They left unforgiven, but You removed condemnation from the accused. Lord, I need that mind-set that releases blame, I who am most guilty of all. Enlarge my heart to welcome the stigmatized and the outcasts. Forgive me. Thank You that You will take me back. Amen.

Day 144

Home Sweet Home

(PSALM 84:1–4)

1 SAMUEL 30–31

JOHN 8:12–47

PSALM 84:1–4

*L*ord Almighty, how lovely is Your dwelling place! You know my multiple addresses. Sometimes it feels like I've had to find a home about as often as the sparrow building her nest every year, and I don't do a good job of maintaining them. Oh, may I not treat Your place with the same disregard. Your house is perfect and beautiful. May I not destroy it by my sin and neglect, starting with my body, Your temple. I cry out for the living God—may I dwell with You forever! I am blessed to live under Your roof. May Your praise be on the tip of my tongue this moment and forever. Amen.

Is It Time?

(2 SAMUEL 2:1–4)

*L*ord God, to have the patience of David. When I see an opening for a long-desired opportunity, I run through. Not David. Even after Your promise, even after Saul died, he still asked, "Is it time for me to go up? To present myself as king?" And knowing David, if You had said not yet, he would have waited. When I pray for something, it's as much about the prayer, our communion, my coming to know You and praise You and worship You in the service of my life, as it is about conducting business at the bank of prayer. You want me to ask about every decision and need—because You want to talk with me. Thank You. Amen.

Day 146

2 Samuel 3–4

John 9:13–34

Psalm 85:1–7

Restore Me Again
(Psalm 85:1–7)

God my Savior, how precious is this prayer. Restore us again. Return me to the place of Your favor when I have fallen away. You've done it before. I have once again squandered Your riches in the wasteland of sin. But in Your amazing grace, Your amazing mercy, I can come before Your mercy seat and beg for forgiveness. I fall before You, pleading, "Revive me again." Fill my heart with Your love. Rekindle my soul with fire from above. Show me Your love. Sanctify me, set me apart, making me more and more like You in the here and now. Amen.

David's Throne

(2 SAMUEL 7:10–16)

---

2 SAMUEL 5:1–7:17

JOHN 9:35–10:10

PSALM 85:8–13

Oh Lord God, to receive Your promise as David did! You only told a handful of people that the Messiah would be one of their direct descendants. How Eve must have rejoiced at the news, after the despair of her sin in the garden. How new, how startling, how marvelous the news came to Abraham, the father of God's chosen people. And then to David, that one of his descendants would rule forever. Last, You told a young, unmarried teenager that her son would be the One. You have a unique message to give to the world in and through me as well. May I shout Your glory aloud. Amen.

Day 148

Listening for His Voice
(John 10:11–30)

2 Samuel 7:18–10:19

John 10:11–30

Psalm 86:1–10

*L*ord Jesus, You are my Shepherd. As Your ewe, I'm supposed to listen to Your voice. Is a sheep like a cat or a dog? My kitties knew my voice. They waited at the front window at the end of the day and ran to the bedroom as soon as I called their names. They raced to me when they heard me but avoided strangers. Lord, may I hear Your voice like that. May I tune my ear to Your station. May I keep myself in range, where I can hear You easily and quickly. When You whisper my name, let me run to You eagerly, so happy You called. Make me like my pets. Amen.

You Are the Man

(2 SAMUEL 12:1–25)

Lord God, how horrible those months must have been for David, after he'd sinned with Bathsheba and killed her husband. Or was he so in love with her that he numbed himself to what he had done? How I rejoice in Nathan's bravery in confronting him, for all the men and women who are unafraid to denounce sin. I pray that when someone points to the log in my eye, I will repent and accept Your corrective surgery. I have seen the sword fall on my family. How I pray that You will spare my grandchildren. They are innocent of past sins. Let me not be defeated today because of the sins of my forebears. Amen.

Day 150

If the Lord Had Been Here

(JOHN 11:17–43)

2 SAMUEL 12:26–13:39

JOHN 11:17–54

PSALM 87

*D*earest Lord, where have You been? If You had been here, my daughter wouldn't have died. Even as I prayed, You comforted me with the image of welcoming her home in heaven, at peace and rest, full of joy. How else do I understand the depth of Your promise of eternal life, except in the pits of despair after the death of a loved one? How I thank You for Your comfort. I praise You for the promise You gave to me through Martha. You are the resurrection and the life. No one who believes in You will ever truly die. Open my heart to receive more of You during those heavy times of grief. Amen.

Morning and Evening
(Psalm 88:1–9)

2 Samuel 14:1–15:12
John 11:55–12:19
Psalm 88:1–9

Lord God, I come to You because You are the One who saves. I don't know how I got into this mess. I'm exhausted and discouraged, lonely and overwhelmed. Morning and evening I cry out to You. Hear my plea in the morning when the day is young and I hope for a good day. Grant me mercy at night when I'm spent and discouraged, seeking rest. I spread my hands open before You, asking You to fill me with goodness. You are my hope, my all-sufficient hope. If there is something holding back Your blessing, show me, convict me. May my faith increase according to my need, for You are always trustworthy. Amen.

Day 152

Flight Prayers

(2 Samuel 15:13–31)

2 Samuel 15:13–16:23
John 12:20–43
Psalm 88:10–18

*H*eavenly Father, even on the run from his own son, David prayed. Oh Lord, give me the grace to approach You in the hardest times. I pray that You will show faithfulness and kindness to the many who have supported me through the years. I seek Your favor both for those who see me face-to-face, in all my petty daily battles, and for those who support me from afar. I ask that Your work will continue unhindered, guiding my steps both away and back again. I need an advocate, someone who will speak up for me and protect me from the harm plotted against me. You are with me, my Rock. Amen.

Jesus Loves Me
(John 13:1–3)

2 Samuel 17:1–18:18
John 12:44–13:20
Psalm 89:1–6

*D*ear Jesus, You knew You were going home. Soon You would regain all the glory You had set aside to come to earth. A part of You must have been thrilled, but still I sense Your sorrow. You loved those disciples and those who would come after them. The days ahead would test everything in them, and You poured every last bit of Yourself into them. Son of God and Son of Man, all authority belongs to You. You could have designated tasks to a million angels. Instead, You washed Your disciples' feet. How much do You love me? You give me a pedicure. Amen.

Contradictions
(2 Samuel 18:19–33)

2 Samuel 18:19–19:39
John 13:21–38
Psalm 89:7–13

*H*eavenly Father, who had turned David's world upside down? A wise man's words disregarded and the king mourning the death of his enemy, his own son—so many of my days are like that, although not usually about such serious matters. For that, I thank You. But almost no days pass without at least one thing jarring the works, stopping things from their usual flow. I want consistency and constancy, familiarity. I don't like change, and my frustration insults those who are trying to change. Forgive me. When my days are in chaos, may I trust in You, the immutable God. Your plan and purpose will never fail. I cling to that, knowing all these other things are secondary to You. Amen.

Continue the Work

(JOHN 14:12–14)

2 SAMUEL 19:40–21:22
JOHN 14:1–17
PSALM 89:14–18

*L*ord Jesus, did I read that right? "*Whoever* believes in me will do the works I have been doing" (John 14:12 NIV, italics added). Not just the apostles who led the way in validating their claims through supernatural events, but *whoever*. The only condition is that I ask for something that will bring glory to the Father. Forgive me when I turn that promise into a religious catchphrase: "In Jesus' name, amen." Make that the prayer of my inner heart. That I will think, speak, act in Your name. When a mighty work is done, may it bring glory to You and the Father and to no one else. In Your name I do pray, amen.

What God Can Do

(2 SAMUEL 22:26–37)

2 SAMUEL 22:1–23:7

JOHN 14:18–15:27

PSALM 89:19–29

*O*h Lord, how I thank You for David's words in the Bible, for his great gifts of imagery that help express my faith better. Of course Your way is perfect. You're God! But I like exploring how it's perfect. You make my feet like a deer's, where I can climb confidently to the highest of Colorado's fourteeners. I find five-pound weights heavy during exercise; You promise to enable me to pull a heavy bronze bow. You've made the path just wide enough for me so I won't slip, nor will I easily get lost. You are the lamp who shines on my way, revealing the steps I take. The more faithful and pure I am, the more I understand of You. Amen.

God Is Truth
(PSALM 89:30–37)

*L*ord God, am I reading this right? That my future sin cannot change Your past covenant? *"In My holiness I cannot lie. I will never stop loving David, never fail to keep My promise to him."* Oh Lord, how I rejoice in that confidence, knowing that although I am changeable, *You* are not, and You won't desert me even when I seem to turn my back on You. Your holiness, Your immutability, Your faithfulness make me the object of Your ever-present, all-compassing love. I don't deserve it, never have, never will; but I offer myself as a living sacrifice of praise. Amen.

Day 158

The Peace Paradox
(JOHN 16:33)

1 KINGS 1
JOHN 16:23–17:5
PSALM 89:38–52

*D*earest Jesus, this paradox can only make sense in You. You tell me I will have trouble in this world, but I will have peace in You. You have overcome the world. Then how is it that trials and sorrows come? I guess overcoming doesn't mean prevention. It means I can withstand the assault, in You, with Your peace. How much comfort it brings me to know that troubles are to be expected. To be reminded not to ask why but how—*how* do I overcome? In You, always in You, by faith, by Your love and peace. Amen.

Praying for Those to Follow
(JOHN 17:20–26)

*Y*ou prayed for me, Lord, at the Last Supper. I bow before You in astonished thankfulness. Such things You asked for me. First I acknowledge the prayer isn't for me, singular; it's for the whole host of people who believe in Your name. You commanded and prayed that we would love one another. Forgive us for falling so far short. You promised Your glory. What a wonder! But none of that happens in a vacuum. You want Your body to stand out in a dark world so that others may come to faith. I pray that will begin here where I live and extend to the farthest reaches of the earth. Amen.

Day 160

All I Ever Wanted

(1 KINGS 3:6–14)

1 KINGS 3–4
JOHN 18:1–27
PSALM 90:13–17

*H*ow exciting, Lord, to see Solomon following in his father's footsteps. His heart must've already been inclined to wisdom to ask for more. He knew he couldn't rule Israel well without guidance. He asked to know the difference between right and wrong. How could he be wise in helping others and so clueless when it came to his own life? But how often am I like that? I can tell others what to do more easily than I can take care of my own problems. As I prepare for the day ahead, let me consider my requests to You. When You ask what I want, let me ask wisely, and not simply for material things. Amen.

What Is Truth?

(JOHN 18:28–40)

1 KINGS 5–6
JOHN 18:28–19:5
PSALM 91:1–10

Dearest Jesus, I bow with You now in this place of life and death, everyone lined up against You and Your closest friends denying You. It's a scary place to be. Even there, You attempted to explain what You were all about, and it feels strange to me that You framed it as "truth." Did Pilate have a clue that You claimed to be the truth? If so, he didn't understand what You meant. I confess I don't understand it completely either. But I trust You as the truth and with my warped perception of reality. Correct my mind to see Your essence more clearly. Amen.

Day 162

Benefits of Loving God
(Psalm 91:11–16)

1 KINGS 7

JOHN 19:6–24

PSALM 91:11–16

Ah, Lord God, what beautiful comfort in these words: *You will rescue those who love You.* You initiated that promise. You will protect those who trust in Your name, in all that is revealed about You by the names You have given Yourself. Even before I call, You are with me in times of trouble. When I call, You are sure to answer. You will bring honor to me. Me?! And You hand me the rewards of a long life and of Your salvation. I am unworthy of any of that. I pray that my love and trust for You will increase. The more of You I know and love, the more blessed I am. Amen.

A Place to Meet with God
(1 Kings 8:1–53)

Lord God, Solomon's prayer reeks of pride. "Look at me, look at this beautiful and glorious temple I've built!" But then he gets down to business. Will You really live on earth? How, since the highest heavens can't contain You? How much more do I ask the same question today. You have said I'm Your temple. You dwell in me. I am a fragile human shell, the only good in me the righteousness that comes from Your Son. Perhaps I'm not meant to "contain" You. You live in me and You spill out of me to others. You are everything I will ever need, everything the whole world needs. Make me an instrument of that promise. Amen.

Warning
(1 Kings 9:1–9)

1 Kings 8:54–10:13
John 20:1–18
Psalm 92:10–15

Lord God, here's where eternal truth is tested in real time. I've been initiated into service as Your temple. I have the glorious promise: I am Your temple. You dwell in me. I am a living sacrifice. You have set me apart as holy. My purpose is to bring honor to Your name. You are watching over me, for I am dear to Your heart. Now for me to live up to that purpose. But woe to me if I fail in following You. You may bring disaster upon disaster on me. May I obey You with integrity and godliness. Forgive me when I fail. Make me a vessel unto honor in Your service. Amen.

Robed in Majesty
(Psalm 93)

1 Kings 10:14–11:43
John 20:19–31
Psalm 93

Oh God the King, You robe Yourself in majesty. Anyone beholding You will immediately recognize Your greatness, Your right to rule. You are armed with strength. You give Your strength to Your soldiers; they don't make You stronger. You sat on Your throne before time began. You are mightier than anything on earth. You must be! You created everything. What You say cannot be undone, Your laws cannot be changed. You reign throughout all eternity. I am but a soldier in Your kingdom, but I wear the colors of Your majesty and Your glory. Your flag goes before me. Amen.

Do I Love You?

(JOHN 21)

1 KINGS 12:1–13:10

JOHN 21

PSALM 94:1–11

Lord Jesus, when You ask me, *"Do you love Me?"* I say I do. But how well will my answer stand up to the kind of probing You put Peter through? Do I love You more than the things surrounding me—my friends, my occupation, all those things I hold dear? I like to think so. But when You come back and ask a second time, a third time, I doubt myself. Forgive me for that part of myself that I hold back. Open my eyes to what I cling to over my love for You. Cleanse me, free me, that I may serve Your sheep in whatever way You call me to. Amen.

To the Ends of the Earth
(ACTS 1:8)

1 KINGS 13:11–14:31
ACTS 1:1–11
PSALM 94:12–23

*L*ord of heaven and earth, everyone knows people who don't believe in You. I pray for those lost sheep, starting with people I see every day and extending across the globe. Wherever Your church is, may we spread the Gospel to our own Jerusalem, Judea, and Samaria, in our neighborhoods, communities, districts, and countries. May we speak in the power of the Holy Spirit to those who haven't heard. Use my single voice, and the chorus of believers, to witness to the nations. Amen.

What Happened to Matthias?

(ACTS 1:12–26)

1 KINGS 15:1–16:20
ACTS 1:12–26
PSALM 95

Lord Jesus, Head of the body, I confess I've never quite understood Matthias's role. We only know he was Your follower from this one mention in Acts, but that tells us so much about him. He was a witness to Your ascension and Your resurrection. He followed You before he was one of the Twelve. Then when he finally had his chance, he still disappeared in silence behind Paul's prominence. He reminds me of how I feel, how many times someone else eclipses me. Teach me that joy comes in serving You, wherever and however You call me, not in any fame or attention that is drawn to me. Amen.

Sing the Glory of the Lord
(Psalm 96:1)

Day 169

1 Kings 16:21–18:19
Acts 2:1–21
Psalm 96:1–8

*L*ord, may each Christian, wherever we live, declare Your glory and Your marvelous deeds to whomever is around us. May all You are and all You've done spring to the lips of all believers everywhere, especially those who live among those who reject their faith. May we never cease to praise You, even when we travel in places where we are uncertain of the reception of Your glory. May Your people speak of You at all times and in all places. Put a song in our hearts. Show me that one person today who needs to hear Your good news. Amen.

Day 170

1 Kings 18:20–19:21
Acts 2:22–41
Psalm 96:9–13

What Are You Doing Here?

(1 Kings 19:9–17)

Lord God Almighty, I should always listen when You speak. When You ask me the same question twice, I had better pay double attention. So what am I doing before You today? Am I like Elijah, feeling like I'm the only one fighting for You and my life is in danger? You talked with him on a regular basis, so what was special about the mountain? Did he need the reminder that a gentle whisper was as powerful as a whirlwind? Perhaps You wanted to quiet his spirit before You stirred the whirlwind of Hazael, Jehu, and Elisha. How thankful I am that just as You met with Elijah on the mountain, You will meet with me today, protect me, save me, and meet my needs. Amen!

The Seat of Fire
(Psalm 97:1–6)

1 Kings 20
Acts 2:42–3:26
Psalm 97:1–6

Oh Lord the King, Your throne sits on a sea of fire. Righteousness and justice are its foundation. Fire goes before You in every place, burning away the dross of evil. None of Your enemies can stand before You. Your fame doesn't just extend to those closest to the throne, but all the way to the farthest reaches of the universe. Heavens and mountains roll away before You, proclaiming Your righteousness, celebrating Your holiness. Let the earth be glad. Let the smallest island in the farthest sea rejoice. Amen.

Day 172

Ahab's Repentance
(1 Kings 21)

1 Kings 21:1–22:28

Acts 4:1–22

Psalm 97:7–12

*L*ord God, what a surprise to discover that evil King Ahab repented. He learned from David, killing Naboth and taking his vineyard. He went on to encourage worship of Amorite gods and did more to lead Your people further away from You than any other king in Israel's history. But when he repented, You listened. You forgave. Your stamp of forgiveness marked his change of heart as genuine. Oh Lord, how I take comfort from that. If You could forgive Ahab and relent from punishing him, how much more can I trust You will forgive me as well, when I repent and believe in Jesus? Forgive me when I stray. Amen.

Praying for Courage
(ACTS 4:23–31)

1 KI. 22:29–2 KI.1
ACTS 4:23–5:11
PSALM 98

Oh Lord, that I might have the heart of those early believers. Peter and John returned from the same court that had crucified Jesus. I might be tempted to pray for protection or to escape their notice. But those first-century followers prayed for courage to speak boldly. I don't face those same severe consequences if I testify, and therefore I have all the more reason to be bold. Compel me to share the good news of Your salvation and all Your wonderful deeds for humankind. May You work among us in such a way that people will recognize Your handiwork. Shake our comfort zones, fill us with Your mighty power, that we may give glory to You. Amen.

Day 174

2 KINGS 2–3

ACTS 5:12–28

PSALM 99

Pick Up Your Mantle
(2 KINGS 2:11–12)

*L*ord, I love the story about Elisha picking up Elijah's mantle. His excitement upon seeing the chariots of fire, his pain at losing his mentor—his willingness to take over. How much of life is like that? Often a new calling comes hand in hand with suffering. My heart is torn in two when I remember the deaths of those dear to me. Only Your power and love keep my heart together where it's breaking. And in that time of loss, do You have a new work for me to do? I rest in the assurance of the protection of the chariots of fire, even when I don't see them. Whatever You ask me to do, You will also prepare me to complete the task. Amen.

Recognizing I Need Help
(ACTS 6:1–7)

God who brought order out of chaos, how often are we like the early church, both personally and corporately. Forgive us when we try to do life on our own. Open our eyes to the times we need help. Lead us to people who are respected and full of spirit and wisdom for areas where we lack experience or talent. Let us work as a team. When someone offers to help me, let me also offer to someone who needs my gifts. As we become one in prayer, love, encouragement, and message, Your truth will spread. Oh Lord, make it so! Amen.

Choosing Friends Carefully
(PSALM 101)

2 KINGS 5:1–6:23

ACTS 7:1–16

PSALM 101

*L*ord God, I start by praising You with songs. I will speak of Your love and justice, and I desire to live blamelessly before You. But do I expect any action on my behalf to earn Your help? It's Your love that makes me worthy. Surround me with people, friends, and helpers who are wise and faithful, above reproach. Let me not cultivate friendships with slanderers or people who are conceited and full of pride. May I not be one of those people. May I be able to stand with Joshua, with David, and say, "As for me and my house, we will serve the Lord." Amen.

Stop and Go
(2 KINGS 6:24–7:2)

2 KINGS 6:24–8:15
ACTS 7:17–36
PSALM 102:1–7

*L*ord God, I almost dislike the uncertainty of not knowing when bad times will end as much as the bad times themselves. There are times I rant against You, like the king's servant, in my desire to have the difficulties resolved. Forgive me for my unbelief, especially when the promise comes from Your trusted servant. May I accept Your promise of deliverance without wavering or doubting. When I am in a time of drought, may I trust in You, only You, to see me through and to bring the drought to an end. Amen.

Day 178

Now and Then

(PSALM 102:8–17)

2 KINGS 8:16–9:37

ACTS 7:37–53

PSALM 102:8–17

*H*eavenly Father, I'm not sure if these verses speak about the earthly Jerusalem, the new Jerusalem, or maybe both. How I thank You for Your promise to David that has brought blessing to people everywhere. Hallelujah! David's promised heir, Jesus, will reign on His throne through all eternity, but He won't be King just of a few thousand square feet in the Middle East. He's King of kings and Lord of lords, both on earth and in heaven. You are there, You have always been there, and You will be there when all memory of today has faded. I love every stone in that kingdom, all the living stones You have placed there. Amen.

The Heavens Opened
(Acts 7:54–60)

Dearest Jesus, what a blessed sight. When Stephen was about to experience the severest test, dying for his faith, You gave him the ultimate vision. He saw You standing by Your Father's right hand. And that testimony cost him his life. How often things seem to work like this, that the times of greatest blessing are also the times of greatest trials. I've protested before. I want to enjoy the blessing unhindered by pain. But why do I think I'm any better than Stephen and so many others? Perhaps You give me that great abundance to hold me up during the trying times. Perhaps it takes pain to recognize what is ultimately important. I thank You that You stand by Your Father's side, interceding for me. Amen.

A Glimmer of Hope
(2 KINGS 13:4–5)

2 KINGS 12–13
ACTS 8:9–40
PSALM 103:1–9

*L*ord God, how much easier it is for my children to learn my poor habits than my good ones. Jeroboam and all his descendants were a bad bunch of rulers. Jeroboam openly and honestly repented, and You cut him some slack. But then his son prayed without repenting. You saved him that one time, but their enemies swarmed back. How I wish I could defeat my besetting sins by one definitive battle, but too often they return to plague me again, and I am forced to call on You again. Show me how to align my life with Your will, to avoid some of the battles. As for the rest—the battle belongs to You. Amen.

Ananias and Saul
(ACTS 9:1–16)

*L*ord Jesus, these verses from Acts take me to holy ground. You performed the impossible, transforming Saul from a death-breathing persecutor to one of the greatest proponents of the Way. And to help that happen, Ananias obeyed You, knowing full well the risks he took. When You direct me to go in a certain direction, may I follow You and share Your words with confidence. Even if I don't get the warm welcome Ananias did, let me take joy from being faithful to Your calling. Only You know the eternal consequences of my actions today. Amen.

All to Thee I Surrender

(Psalm 103:15–22)

2 Kings 16–17

Acts 9:17–31

Psalm 103:15–22

Let all that I am praise You, Lord. Let all my heart, all my soul, all my strength—everything I am and hope to be—praise You. Let me bless You, lift Your name on high. Let gratitude and affection flow from every pore of my being toward You. You are Yahweh, the great I Am, the eternal God. You are Adonai, my Lord Master. You are worthy of all the praise I have to offer, and so much more. May I devote every fiber of my being to praising You. May I join the worldwide chorus in offering praise at Your throne. Amen.

Rooftop Prayers
(ACTS 10)

2 KINGS 18:1–19:7
ACTS 9:32–10:16
PSALM 104:1–9

Father God, how appropriate that Peter would be on the rooftop praying when You announced that the good news was meant for Gentiles as well as Jews. How precious to know Peter wasn't alone in his prayers. Cornelius had also been petitioning You. In the middle of the afternoon, no less—the middle of a workday for a Roman centurion. You brought together these two bold, brave men who might have clashed in any other circumstances, and made them brothers in You. You'll shake up my prayers from time to time. May I listen as well as talk, that I may hear what Your calling is for today. Use me to increase Your kingdom here on earth. Amen.

Day 184

Show Them

(2 KINGS 19:14–19)

2 KINGS 19:8–20:21

ACTS 10:17–33

PSALM 104:10–23

*H*eavenly Father, You know I have a Sennacherib whispering falsehoods in my ear, just as he did to Hezekiah. Teach me to be as wise as Hezekiah in dealing with it. Oh, deafen me, blind me, to the enemies' claims that they are greater than You. I know the claims are false, from a lifetime of practice and study, but I suspect I could easily fall prey to lies. Whenever I am tempted to doubt, teach me to come to You, asking You to act once again. Strut Your stuff. Remind my enemies they are but pawns in the greatest chess game of eternity, and You are King and Queen and Knight to control and protect. Amen.

Memory vs. Record
(2 Kings 22)

2 Kings 21–22
Acts 10:34–11:18
Psalm 104:24–30

Wonderful Counselor, I need You these days more than ever, when I can't depend on my memory any longer. Forgive me when I fall into a routine of how I think things are supposed to be done. I think I remember it very clearly. Then I do housecleaning, read an old email, discover an old journal—and it's not so. What a shock to Josiah's helpers when they cleaned the temple. They thought they had been doing things right until they read Your Word again. Give me a teachable spirit and a desire to share what I learn with others, that together we may ever obey You with fuller understanding. Amen.

Day 186

A Mutual Love Fest

(PSALM 104:31–35)

2 KINGS 23

ACTS 11:19–12:17

PSALM 104:31–35

*L*ord God, as one doctrinal statement puts it, the chief end of man is to glorify and enjoy You forever. You created me and all people for relationship. You looked on Your creation—people!—and called us very good. Whenever I praise You, You are already rejoicing over me with singing. Like a child, I sit on Your lap, and we play a game of who-loves-whom-the-most. There is no real comparison, of course, but You take great pleasure in hearing my voluntary expressions of adoration, and You cherish those intimate times when You have my full attention. Why would I ever turn away from a time like that? Amen.

Your Praise on My Lips
(PSALM 105:1–7)

2 KINGS 24–25
ACTS 12:18–13:13
PSALM 105:1–7

Lord God, may Your praise be on my lips for all eternity. Your name is so grand, so glorious, that I have only halting words to speak of it. I rhapsodize about the miracle of creation and revel in Your judgments, testing them to be right and true. I scroll through my scrapbook of memories of Your wonderful acts. The title on each page sums the experience. All I have to do is say "Christmas 1982" and the miraculous way You provided for us that year floods my mind. May I sing, write, and speak of Your wonderful acts in my life and the world in every way I can to every person I can. Amen.

Day 188

Any News?
(ACTS 13:14–43)

1 CHRONICLES 1–2

ACTS 13:14–43

PSALM 105:8–15

*H*eavenly Father, did anyone at that worship service at Antioch of Pisidia have any idea what was happening? The first sermon on Paul's first missionary journey, and wow, what a story he had to tell. Jesus Son of David sounds more like a Wild West legend than a truthful account, and yet the listeners heard and wanted to know more. Lord, open my ears to discern truth from falsehood. May I be driven to speak Your Word boldly, as Paul was. When I communicate, may people hear Your truth. Not only for me, but I pray also for those who go to places where people haven't heard of You or have forgotten. Amen.

1 Chronicles 3:1–5:10

Acts 13:44–14:10

Psalm 105:16–28

Lord God, I want to be like Jabez. He didn't wait for relief from pain before he went to work. Instead he went to work. He asked You to take him from where he was to where You wanted him to be. Forgive me for the times I let my circumstances hold me back from following You with all my heart. May I rely on the arms You place around me when I'm ready to give up, fatigued. You have work for me to do, supernatural work that I can only do through Your power and strength. May I return everything You give me as an offering of praise. Amen.

Family Business

(1 CHRONICLES 6:48)

1 CHR. 5:11–6:81
ACTS 14:11–28
PSALM 105:29–36

*L*ord God, how does this concept of a family business that extends for multiple generations apply today? Aaron and his descendants were priests before You forever. The other Levites were given specific duties. *Where is free choice in such an arrangement?* my modern sensibilities protest. Then I see my son and how he shares many of my passions, strengths, and weaknesses. That although his life follows a different pattern than mine, we both are drawn to serve You in similar ways. It's both nature and nurture and, most importantly, Your calling and gifting. Whatever that calling is, give me the grace to obey and follow it with my whole heart. Amen.

Coming to a Consensus

1 CHRONICLES 7:1–9:9
ACTS 15:1–18
PSALM 105:37–45

*H*eavenly Father, I hate it when I disagree with my brothers and sisters in Christ. How often we have a difference of opinion in our interpretation of Your Word because of our mind-sets. We can't see there's another way to look at it. We bring our culture, religious training, and language to Your Word. No wonder Jews and Gentiles came into conflict. How I need Your mind, that I might ponder soundly, consider things as You would, rather than as a twenty-first century white woman would. Give me a glimpse of Your truth, and enable me to pass it on to others without offending. Amen.

Day 192

Breathing You
(Psalm 106:1–3)

1 Chr. 9:10–11:9

Acts 15:19–41

Psalm 106:1–12

*B*oth now and through all eternity, let us praise You, oh Lord. For You are good and You have done great things, greater than the grandest epics captured by human tongue. I ask You for more "Hallelujah Chorus" moments when I stand to my feet in awe, in praise, for more times when I stumble and bow, swept up in a worship song. May I never tire of the old, old story, because its power continues without pause or alteration, always run by Your love. Make me one who acts justly and who does what is right. I want the privilege of singing in that heavenly chorus. Amen.

Macedonian Call
(ACTS 16:6–10)

1 CHR. 11:10–12:40
ACTS 16:1–15
PSALM 106:13–27

*O*h Lord Jesus, I sit in Your presence, rejoicing that Paul responded to the cry of the man from Macedonia to go over and help him. When Paul stepped onto the continent of Europe, You thought of me and all the others from that day until now. I am building a monument of thanksgiving at this place, but perhaps You are calling me elsewhere. Give me vision to seek and ears to hear that one person who is eager and ready to receive the good news. Cause our paths to cross and Your name to spring from my lips. Make me visible and verbal with my faith. Amen.

Day 194

A Threesome

(PSALM 106:30–31)

1 CHR. 13–15
ACTS 16:16–40
PSALM 106:28–33

*L*ord God, thank You for the vow You made with Phinehas for a lasting priesthood. Just as there was Abraham, Isaac, and Jacob to father the line of the promise, so here You chose Aaron, Eleazar, and Phinehas to intercede for the people of Israel. Phinehas acted boldly for Your honor, in ways that make me uncomfortable. Does the possibility of drastic action hold me back from total commitment? You've given me a ministry of grace and reconciliation. I ask for two things: that You will provide me with a circle of three godly people to lift one another up, and that I will act without hesitation in whatever fashion You direct when sin strikes our heels. Amen.

A Map for Musicians
(1 Chronicles 16)

*O*h God who is most worthy of praise, I read this official hymn given to the temple musicians and revel in all the emotions and activities of worship. May my times before You, both by myself and with others, reflect the same values. May I proclaim Your name among the nations, making known what You have done. When we sing, may we bring glory to Your name. Give me a heart to seek You, and not just one to glance up and see if You're around. May we tell in song of Your wonderful history with the sons of men. Amen!

Day 196

1 Chr. 18–20

Acts 17:15–34

Psalm 106:44–48

Oh Lord, how glorious to know that You're working behind the scenes. Sometimes You use people to discipline me; other times You use them to show me Your mercy. And You wish to do the same in me, with me, through me. Perhaps there is someone You want to bless through me. Forgive me when I criticize the person You wish to encourage. Use the words I write and speak to build others up. May they comfort others in the same way I've been comforted. Speak to me through them. The same Holy Spirit lives in all of us. May we together give thanks to Your name and praise Your glory. Amen.

David's Mistakes

*H*eavenly Father, how glad I am that David's life is recorded in the Bible, including his mistakes, even in his later years. If You could love a man who kept making a mess, I dare hope You will love me. In his repentance, I see his wisdom has grown with his age. His sin was his responsibility, his alone, and he refused to allow anyone else to pay for it. He certainly didn't want to take this poor man's farm for free, the way he killed Uriah, and I thank You that however horrible my past mistakes, I don't have to stay that way. You will continue molding me into the image of Christ until the day You call me home. Amen.

Day 198
———

1 Chr. 23–25
Acts 18:24–19:10
Psalm 107:10–16

Teachable Spirit
(Acts 18:24–28)

*L*ord God, I pray for discernment and a teachable spirit. Show me the difference between false teaching and differing interpretations. Let me embrace differences with grace but correct where there is falsehood. When You bring an Apollo into my life, let me speak Your words, and let Your Spirit draw me and those I am conversing with together in love and unity. Give me the grace to encourage those You've given me to lead along the way with wisdom and patience. Let me also listen and learn from those who are farther down the road than I am. May we work together to build up Your church. Amen.

1 Chr. 26–27
Acts 19:11–22
Psalm 107:17–32

*D*ivine Healer, more prayer requests are asked for healing than for anything else. Teach me how to pray. Today I bring before You all who are sick. I pray for those whose unwise or sinful ways have led to their illness, that You will heal them in spirit and body. I pray for those with disabilities, whether from birth or from accident, that You would bring them to all fullness, whatever that looks like. Oh Creator of mind and body, heal those with mental illness. Rework the patterns of their minds. For those nearing death, I ask that they will first of all be saved and then that they will have peace and strength, choosing to live each day to the fullest. Amen.

Choose Your God Here

(ACTS 19:23–41)

1 CHR. 28–29
ACTS 19:23–41
PSALM 107:33–38

*L*ord God, it's disturbing to live in a culture where Christians are rejected because they claim there is only one way to God. But Paul ran into the same problem in Ephesus. Now as then, people want to choose their own deity. How foolish it would be to hold a straw poll to determine whom to worship. Who wants a God who needs an election before taking office, who could be deposed in twelve months? Such a god is no more than I am, hopeless to solve the world's problems. You are God. Period. Thank You for giving me the eyes to see now before the day You force everyone to acknowledge You. May I share the truth of the One true God with love and grace. Amen.

Why Them, Not Me?
(2 Chronicles 2)

2 Chr. 1–3
Acts 20:1–16
Psalm 107:39–43

My Lord God, it seems strange that Solomon chose unbelieving foreigners to build the temple. Did Hiram believe in You? He acknowledged You as the creator God. What about the foreigners who were conscripted for labor? Were they people whom You had drawn to Yourself, blessed with the opportunity of a lifetime—to build a temple for You? Did Jewish builders wonder why they were overlooked? Forgive me when I envy the assignments You give to others. You've given me a long list of gifts and opportunities, but I still lust for the one fruit remaining on the branch. Forgive me. Use us together to bring glory to You. Amen.

Day 202

Saying Goodbye

(ACTS 20:17–38)

2 CHR. 4:1–6:11
ACTS 20:17–38
PSALM 108

*H*eavenly Father, throughout my life, I've had to say farewells, whether I am the one leaving or being left. May I be as gracious in my goodbyes as Paul was. May my record be as consistent as Paul's was—humble, up-front, personal, unprejudiced. Where I have failed in the past, correct me now. May my goal with my peers be to share the good news of Your Son, my Lord and Savior Jesus Christ. May all of us together commit ourselves to finishing the race of faith strong; may all of us together sing of Your salvation. Amen.

God's Resting Place
(2 Chronicles 6:12–42)

Acts 21:1–14
Psalm 109:1–20

*L*ord God, Solomon and I wrestled with the same questions. You are God. You can't be contained by Your creation. I'm the smallest Who in Whoville, calling for help. And glory be! You hear me! May Your praises ring the rafters and explode the ceiling—until the news of Your love and salvation spreads from my ears to my neighbors, to my city, and across the earth. May I join with other believers to pray. If my individual cries for help are heard, how much more glorious when they're joined by throngs of others? Amen.

Day 204

2 CHR. 7:11–9:28
ACTS 21:15–32
PSALM 109:21–31

In Pain

Sovereign God, how often the song in my mouth is the prayer in my heart. My prayers turn to You. Where else would I go? You are good. Your love never fails. Your name stands higher than all others. I'm a weak and needy sinner approaching You for help. I've wandered in the darkness of my sin until I'm stretched thin, hardly more than a Gollum in the story of my life. But on that dark journey, You hear my plea for help and deliverance. You bless me and uplift me in the presence of my enemies. I thank You for the storms You've brought me through. Let me extol Your name forever. Amen.

What Are You Waiting for?

Day 205

(ACTS 22:14–16)

2 CHR. 9:29–12:16
ACTS 21:33–22:16
PSALM 110:1–3

*T*his hits me square on the chin, Lord. *What am I waiting for?* I come to You, begging for directions. I'm so tired, the task I've been given seems so impossible, my tools so inadequate, that I keep asking for additional help. But what do I think I need? You've already saved me, my future in heaven is secure, and You've given me a task. The time has come for me to stop asking and to start acting on what I know, getting right with You, getting right with others. You will answer when I call as I go about Your business. Amen.

Safe Passage
(ACTS 23:11)

2 CHR. 13–15
ACTS 22:17–23:11
PSALM 110:4–7

*D*ear Jesus, I thank You for Paul's obedience in following Your will, even when he knew it meant imprisonment and possibly death. I just wish the Bible told us more about why he felt compelled to return to Jerusalem. Do You plan for my faith walk to be like that? To pursue a dangerous future without any obvious confirmation that it's of You? May I listen and obey, whether You shout from heaven or simply brush my spirit. How precious Your promise, that You gave Your blessing after he obeyed and was imprisoned. You fulfilled his desire to testify in Rome as well. Charm my inner being so my greatest desires lie in the direction of Your will. Amen.

Honoring Teachers
(2 Chronicles 17:7–10)

Day 207

2 Chr. 16–17
Acts 23:12–24:21
Psalm 111

*O*h heavenly Father, to have a leader like King Jehoshaphat. It's never too late for a person or nation to repent and follow You. Thank You for his wisdom in sending out his best staff to teach Your Word to the people. How little I know of Ben-Hail, Shemaiah, Elishama, and others, but I thank You for their faithfulness to You and to their earthly king. How heartily they must have studied Your Word to be able to teach it. How You must have transformed their lives. And through them, You transformed the nation. If I can do as the least of them did, I will be a woman of God. That is my prayer, to encourage and teach. Amen.

Day 208

Praying for My Children
(Psalm 112)

2 Chr. 18–19

Acts 24:22–25:12

Psalm 112

*P*raise You, Lord. Praise Your holy name. I lift up my children, my family, to You. Before I pray for Your blessings, Lord, I beseech You for their character. May they fear You and delight in You. May they be gracious and compassionate in their interactions with people, just and generous in their dealings. I pray that You will keep them close to You, that You will make them mighty and secure, blessed in spirit and in material things, that they will come to You as their Savior and receive Your righteousness forever. Amen.

Valley of Blessing
(2 CHRONICLES 20:25)

2 CHR. 20–21
ACTS 25:13–27
PSALM 113

Wonderful Counselor, You are the fount of all comfort, the Creator of my mind, the original and best therapist to me where I'm broken. Help me to unlock the door of my fortress and walk into the fullness You have waiting for me. I've been living on the edge, making unhealthy choices because I see no other way to survive. Forgive me! Remove the scales from my eyes. Shatter the walls of my self-made fortress. Open me to the available abundance instead of the rubbish where I've been living. Life in my valley can be richer than the thin air on the mountaintop. Amen.

Athaliah and Jehosheba

(2 Chronicles 22–23)

2 Chr. 22–23

Acts 26

Psalm 114

*L*ord God, what a scary story—with one ambitious woman throwing the kingdom into upheaval, and another acting with great love and courage to sweep an infant straight out of the royal nursery to safety. As much as I want to be Jehosheba the heroine, at times I display characteristics of the ambitious, murderous Athaliah. Forgive me! Safeguard my mind and heart from jealousy. How easy it is to go from wanting what someone else has to taking it from them. Strike the thoughts from me. Whatever ministry or gifts You have given to me, let me share them with others without pause. Use me to guide those beginners. Amen.

To God Be the Glory
(PSALM 115:1–10)

Lord God, to Your name, not mine, be the glory. Make me into a mirror, like the moon, that whatever glory hits me will reflect back to You, that my craters and darkness may fade away and people see only Your shining glory. May they see Your faithfulness and abundant love in the brilliance of Your acts. May I not seek a name for myself but for You. When people think of me, let them remember all the wonderful things You've done on my behalf. When I'm afraid, when I'm blind, let me trust in that glory, love, and faithfulness. You are my help and my shield. You surround me and protect me. Amen.

Day 212

2 CHR. 25:17–27:9
ACTS 27:21–28:6
PSALM 115:11–18

Islands

(ACTS 27:21–41)

*O*h God to whom I belong, I come before You in the midst of a tremendous storm. A small band sails alone on treacherous seas. You know my heart, that I look forward to going home but believe You have work yet for me to do. Oh, thank You for the reassurance that Your calling is sure! It will happen, maybe not how I pictured it. Like Paul, a prisoner, I'm not alone in the squall. I pray for the lives of everyone around me. I pray that no one with me will be given over to destruction. Use me to encourage those around me to endure and survive life's shipwrecks together. Amen.

Not My Father
(2 Chronicles 28–29:19)

*L*oving Father, I can't wrap my head around a father who would sacrifice the son of his own body to a god of fire. What a stench it must have made to Your nostrils. How I thank You for Hezekiah's testimony. He broke the pattern of generational sin. Oh, to live like him, where he made his first order of business to repair the broken places. How I rejoice in not having to be defined by my parents, and I pray the same for my children. How thankful I am for the things they have done well. Make me a Hezekiah in my time and before my children, and not an Ahaz. Amen.

Day 214

A Reputation like Rome's
(ROMANS 1:7–10)

2 CHR. 29:20–30:27
ROMANS 1:1–17
PSALM 116:6–19

My reputation, Lord. What is it? What do the people I know, from my neighbors to people who have never met me in person, think of me? Forgive me when my flame spreads muddy ash instead of burning brightly for You. Make me like the believers in Rome. Thank You that You have called me as part of Your holy people. I pray that whenever other people think of me, they will think of You. That I will play some part, however small, in spreading the good news of Your salvation across the earth. And lead me to fellowship with others who are Your called, wherever they are from. Amen.

All You Peoples
(PSALM 117)

God of the universe, the heavenly host, and all mankind—I add my voice to the throng. Whenever we gather, two or three together, let us add our prayers, cries, and praise to the church universal. May we join our petitions with the persecuted church, with those living without freedom of religion. You reign, and my prayers rise up to You along with those of every tribe and tongue. How I look forward to the day when we will all understand one another's speech. You are great and Your faithfulness never fails. You are the only One greater than we ourselves. Amen.

Day 216

Your Love Never Quits

(PSALM 118:1–18)

2 CHR. 33:1–34:7
ROMANS 2
PSALM 118:1–18

*L*oving God, I'm running to You, crawling if that's all the strength I have. Because now, this morning, there is a fresh supply of Your compassion. Your faithfulness will never expire or be out-of-date. You'll never hang an OUT OF STOCK sign on Your door and turn me away. I'm sticking with You. From the wide-open spaces of eternity You come to me in my here and now. My life seems to hang by a thread and the enemy's scissors are closing in. My Rock, my Shelter, come to my aid. Cover me in the shadow of Your wings until I am strong enough to stand. Amen.

The Haves and Have-Nots
(ROMANS 3:1–26)

Oh Lord God, I was once lost but now am found. I once was a sinner, a mouse trying to jump over the moon of Your holiness, the distance too far for me to travel in a million lifetimes. And yet, incredibly, I am righteous, justified, transformed by Your Son's atoning blood. No matter how often I repeat the good news, I still tremble at the law I spurned and rest in Your amazing grace. Whatever separates me from other believers, this brings us back together. Thrust apart by sin, brought together by grace. Make it so in the places we brush against each other. Amen.

Today Is the Day
(Psalm 118:24)

2 Chr. 35:20–36:23

Romans 3:27–4:25

Psalm 118:24–29

*T*oday is the time to praise You. It's the only day I have. I can't make up for what I didn't do yesterday or store up praise for tomorrow. This is the day You have made, and therefore it is good and fitting, Your gift to me to turn back as an offering to You, every minute a new beginning. You not only made today and gave it to me; You also are acting in my now, on my behalf. Oh, let me join my voice with other believers to say, "This is the day which the Lord hath made; we will rejoice and be glad in it" (Psalm 118:24). Amen.

Hope Is My Middle Name
(ROMANS 5:1–5)

God of all comfort, thank You for all the ways hope works in my life. I hope while I'm suffering, because I know You won't leave me stranded but will always rescue me and set me on a rock. You keep me safe. You are present with me in my trials. Hope fills me with Your love. Without troubles, how could I know of Your deliverance? If I don't recognize Your tender care in the depths, how will I recognize it in the heights? I boast of that hope and all the wonderful things You have for me. Amen.

Day 220

EZRA 4–5

ROMANS 6:1–7:6

PSALM 119:9–16

Sanctify Me

(ROMANS 6)

*L*ord and Master, with each passing moment, remind me that I have a choice because I am no longer under the law and the power of sin, but under grace. Make me an instrument of righteousness. Bring that choice to my mind when I'm the most tired, the most likely to let sin rule. Let me test the fruit of my choices, that I may judge them accurately. Have I chosen what appeals to my eyes, my fleshly desires? Or have I lifted my eyes like Isaiah to see You in Your majesty and holiness? Cleanse me of sin and impurity. Renew my spirit. Amen.

God of Heaven
(Ezra 6)

Ezra 6:1–7:26
Romans 7:7–25
Psalm 119:17–32

*G*od of heaven, when people look back on today, will they see Your hand at work as clearly as I see it in Bible times? Make it so. Like Darius, I worship You, the God of heaven. I praise You that in these latter days You have caused Your name to dwell both in the grandeur of the heavens and in the flesh of Your Son, full of grace and glory. I pray today for our leaders, for their well-being, for Your wisdom to fall on them as they lead us. Like Darius, may they recognize You. Amen.

Day 222

Ezra 7:27–9:4
Romans 8:1–27
Psalm 119:33–40

Not Asking for Help
(Ezra 8:21–23)

Gracious God, how I thank You for the many times You send aid from the hands of Your children and even from unbelievers. I stand in awe of Ezra's faith. He refused to ask for help because he had bragged that Your hand was on everyone who looked to You. Forgive me if my doubt brings shame on Your name. I humble myself before You, for I am nothing, and ask You for a safe journey from now to the end of my days. Great God of heaven above, how I thank You that You hear and answer my prayer. Amen.

Daily Walk
(PSALM 119:41–64)

Day 223

EZRA 9:5–10:44
ROMANS 8:28–39
PSALM 119:41–64

*H*eavenly Father, I am physically pained, mentally fatigued, and discouraged. Remember Your Word to me, for my hope is in Your unfailing love. Every day You offer a new batch of compassion, and I trust Your history of faithfulness. From the days when I first came to know You, oh God, I've believed Your promise that forgiveness requires only simple, honest confession and repentance. But willfulness and rebellion make my faults stick in my throat. Though I ache to admit them, they hold me. Free me, Savior, to open my soul to You. May my heart run to You to seek Your pardon. Cleanse me from all sin, and glorify Yourself in my life. Amen.

Hardened Hearts
(ROMANS 9:18)

NEH. 1:1–3:16
ROMANS 9:1–18
PSALM 119:65–72

Sovereign Lord, as Your daughter, I tumble with laughter and tears into Your lap. How grateful I am that You had mercy on me, on my family, and on so many who are near and dear to me. I am saddened when I see people who refuse You repeatedly. Is that when You harden their hearts? Is that what happens to those nations of the earth, those who are most resistant to the good news, Your own special people, the Jews, chosen by You? Oh, how I beseech You that the scales will fall from their eyes! You don't want any to perish. Break apart those bars of iron on darkened hearts. Amen.

The Results of Meditation
(PSALM 119:73–80)

NEH. 3:17–5:13
ROMANS 9:19–33
PSALM 119:73–80

Oh Lord, how wonderful to read of the power of Your Word. It's not simply meant to tickle my ears. May it change me. Because I hope in Your Word, may others rejoice. Because Your laws are righteous, convict me of my sin. I find comfort in Your promises. Your compassion gives me light as I delight in Your law. The better I understand Your statutes, the more prepared I am to teach others. May I meditate on Your precepts and follow Your decrees with all my heart and soul, that I might not shame Your name. Amen.

Strengthen My Hands
(Nehemiah 6:9)

Neh. 5:14–7:73
Romans 10:1–13
Psalm 119:81–88

My Lord God, when enemies taunt me, saying I can't finish the work, strengthen my hands. When foes accuse me for the wrong reasons or of unfair tactics, pour purpose into my actions. If people speak against me in the name of God, turn it back on them. When the days seem long and the task seems harsh, steady my hands. When I am faint, when I doubt the work I'm engaged in, renew my vision, that I may renew my commitment. When I feel alone in the work, bring helpmates to labor beside me. And when the task is done, may I return all glory and praise to You. Amen.

How Shall They Hear?
(ROMANS 10:14–15)

NEH. 8:1–9:5
ROM. 10:14–11:24
PSALM 119:89–104

Lord Jesus, the irrefutable logic stirs me from the bottom of my heart. People who haven't heard of You can't call on You, and they can't hear without a preacher. How I thank You again that I grew up in a land where Your Word is abundantly spoken. I beg You, make me both a preacher and a sender. Make the wheels on my chair and my fingers on computer keys beautiful as I write and speak of Your wondrous salvation. May I also play my role in sending preachers to those who haven't heard. May the day come ever nearer when every tribe and tongue and nation has heard. Amen.

Day 228

Trifling Hardship?
(NEHEMIAH 9:6–37)

NEH. 9:6–10:27

ROMANS 11:25–12:8

PSALM 119:105–120

Lord God, what a bold prayer! Thank You for the Levites' example to bring even my trifling problems to You. You are the highest God of the highest heaven, from the depths of the sea to the far ends of the universe, so how is it that You see me? I'm just a pebble upon which my troubles are dust, and yet You know the weight of them on me. Oh, I fall in worship and thanksgiving. You are a forgiving God, gracious and compassionate, slow to anger and abounding in love. Your Spirit instructs me in all matters, great and small. I praise You and thank You. Amen.

Coal Bearer
(ROMANS 12:20–21)

Day 229

NEH. 10:28–12:26
ROMANS 12:9–13:7
PSALM 119:121–128

Lord Jesus, as a pale imitation of Your sacrifice, You tell me to feed my enemies, to care for them, until the coals You've placed in my hands burn away the hostility between us as well as between them and You. Make me a coal bearer today. Use those burning coals to purify me and to draw my enemies closer to You, no matter how painful. How often I feel overcome by the circumstances of living in a fallen and imperfect world. Make me a force for good. Let me be an inspiration and not a drain on those around me. Amen.

Day 230

Keep Me from Sin
(Psalm 119:129–136)

iving Word, You are the Light of the World, and Your wonderful words give light. May I never wander beyond the reach of Your light. I pant for Your words, hungry for the righteousness and truth they provide. They show me the way I should walk and keep my feet from slipping. Direct my footsteps according to Your Word, that I might not sin. And when I do sin, have mercy on me. Your lovely name speaks of Your abundant love and forgiveness. Let not the sins of those around me turn me away from You. I pray not only for myself, but also for all who need this prayer. Forgive us, Lord. Amen.

Different Is Okay
(Romans 14:13–15:13)

Esther 1:1–2:18
Rom. 14:13–15:13
Psalm 119:137–152

Our Lord and Savior, may I join together with other Christians, even if our practices differ. Together we ask You to fill us with joy and peace, that we may overflow with hope in the Holy Spirit. Our unity comes from You, not from the exact things we eat or the way we dress. Teach me, humble me, to not judge others whose theology and values differ from mine. Let me not create a stumbling block for someone else by my behavior, but rather live in such a way that leads to building each other up toward good works. Amen.

Day 232

Perfect Peace
(PSALM 119:165)

ESTHER 2:19–5:14
ROMANS 15:14–21
PSALM 119:153–168

*D*ear Lord, how I hunger for peace. I crave an inner peace that keeps me on an even keel. Make my outside calm, with my faith planted in the ground of Your faithfulness, so that I won't stumble. Prince of Peace, rule me inside and out as I struggle with daily life and health issues. Let my passion for Your Word fill my body, soul, and spirit. Loosen the grip of temptations on my life; show me how to live in peace in spite of my weaknesses. For in You, when I am weak, then I am strong. Amen.

When God's Favor Means Fighting
(ESTHER 8)

ESTHER 6–8
ROMANS 15:22–33
PSALM 119:169–176

Lord God, Your hand is so evident in Esther's narrative. You gave Mordecai opportunities within the palace, made Esther queen, and gave her favor when she sought the king's help. But when it came down to Your solution, they still had to fight. I shouldn't be surprised when that happens. I pray, asking a way out of the dangerous situation. When the battle comes upon me, I wonder if You failed to answer my prayer. Open my eyes to the weapon You've placed in my hands. Train my hands to fight. Remind me that You don't always spare me the battle, but You will always give me victory. Amen.

Day 234

Mountain-High Help

(PSALM 121)

ESTHER 9–10

ROMANS 16

PSALM 120–122

*M*aker of heaven and earth, what comfort and courage I take from Your words. Stand guard over me when I walk in Your way. You won't let me fall down. Your attention is constantly upon me; You have no need of rest. You even provide shade from the burning sun and hide me from my enemies. You watch over me, both when I go out to work and when I come home, in the intimate details of my family life. I look to the grandeur of the mountains because they remind me of how much greater You are. Amen.

Grief
(JOB 1:20)

O h Father, when tragedy strikes, may I show the same wisdom and faith as Job. He grieved first, throwing himself into mourning rituals. May I never feel ashamed of my feelings, but like Job, may I bring them to You. May I, like him, thank You for the gift of those so near and dear to me, especially my daughter who is now dead. And just as You gave her to me for a short time, You called her home. It is all through You and for You. May Your name be praised in my grief even as I praised You at her birth. Through it all, may I trust in You. Amen.

God Helps the Needy

(JOB 5:15–16)

JOB 4–6

1 COR. 1:26–2:16

PSALM 124–125

*H*eavenly Father, how thankful I am for Job's example. His faith remained strong when You stripped him of his riches and health. He remained committed to You when he was poor. He knew that You still cared for him as You care for the poor and needy. I pray for the needy around me, for children who are abandoned, neglected, abused. God, rescue them! I pray for those in nursing homes, whose minds wander and who feel the pangs of loneliness. Protect them; ease their spirits. For those who are refugees in war-torn lands, oh, shut the mouth of injustice so that they might have hope. I pray for Your strong arm of comfort for the grieving. Show me what role You want me to play in their lives. Amen.

Job 7–9

1 Corinthians 3

Psalm 126–127

*L*ord Jesus, You are the cornerstone of the church, and I am Your temple. As unlikely as it was that You would dwell in a temple made of wood and stone, how much less that You would live in a child born of sin? But You redeemed me, purified me, and now You dwell in me. Let me be careful about what I use to build on that foundation: gold and silver or hay and wood. You live in me. Transform my thoughts, that I may better understand. Mold me into Your likeness. With all Christians, may we reflect the fullness of You. Amen.

Day 238

--------○◯ʂ

JOB 10–13

1 COR. 4:1–13

PSALM 128–129

Hope in the Depths

(JOB 11:18)

*H*eavenly Father, You have given me the ultimate security of salvation and Your indwelling Spirit, the environment of Your never-failing love. Thank You for planting that hope in my heart! When I overcome obstacles or I'm optimistic, it's because of the hope You have given me. When I'm restless during the night, troubled by the events of the day, shine Your light into the darkness of my soul and remind me that You are my safety net, my secure tower. I can rest in peace. Without You, I am nothing. With You, I have everything I will ever need. Thank You. Praise You! Forgive my doubts. Amen.

Waiting with Bated Breath
(PSALM 130)

Day 239

JOB 14–16
1 COR. 4:14–5:13
PSALM 130

*H*eavenly Father, I'm waiting with bated breath, pregnant with anticipation, fainting from thirst and hunger, as desperate as a junkie in need of a fix, as tired as a worker waiting for their relief to show up. As wakeful as I am, wishing I could sleep, I wait for You. I can't let go—I won't let go—for with You there is unfailing love, full redemption, and peace. My hope comes from You. I'm not looking for salvation from any other corner. You are the morning star, the harbinger of my hope. You never have, never will, and never can disappoint. You always deliver on Your promises. Your guarantee is more important than anything else I'm hoping for. Amen.

Day 240

A Weaned Infant
(Psalm 131:1–2)

Job 17–20

1 Corinthians 6

Psalm 131

*L*oving Father, I want to be like the person in this psalm, knowing contentment like that of a weaned child, the continual reassurance that I am loved and special. Help me to grow into that independence. I want to change from a demanding infant to a child who confidently runs to You but leaves and plays, satisfied to know You are near. May I live and work under the shadow of Your wings, secure and confident. Like a child, keep me from worrying about matters too wonderful for me. I seek to know You, to become more like You, my Father. Amen.

Being Single
(1 CORINTHIANS 7:1–16)

JOB 21–23
1 COR. 7:1–16
PSALM 132

*H*eavenly Father, I thank You that I have enjoyed both the joys of marriage and the blessings of the single life. I pray for those believers who are single like me. That if it is Your will, You will bring a spouse that's a perfect fit for us. If not, then let us be at peace and rejoice in our calling. Let us pursue You with all our heart and give doubly of ourselves. For those who are single parents, grant them a double measure of grace as they do a job You designed for two people to carry. I pray for increased understanding and support for single adults among our churches. Amen.

Day 242

JOB 24–27
1 COR. 7:17–40
PSALM 133–134

Understanding God
(JOB 26:13–14)

Lord God, we see Your hand at work in nature—in each day's sunrise, in the physical properties of earth and sky, in growing plants and animals that live and breathe, with man at the apex. And yet all that is only the flaming edges of Your glory. Our sin can't obscure You totally, only present a partial eclipse of all You are. When You burst through that darkness, when You strike in Your mighty power, who can withstand You? Open my eyes to see Your handiwork in the beating of a hummingbird's wings. Forgive me when I fail to acknowledge Your rightful place. Amen.

Reasons to Praise

(PSALM 135)

JOB 28–30
1 CORINTHIANS 8
PSALM 135

We praise You, oh Lord, in the sanctuary. We praise You at our home altars. Let all who minister before You praise You. Let all who share a love for the name of Jesus with me join me in praise. For You are great, greater than anything we have ever seen, and I long to hear the testimony of others about You. I've felt You in the mountains. Let me hear from those who've met You in the rainforests and in the deserts. Let us together remember the great things You've done for Your people and take hope for today. Your name endures forever and Your compassion for eternity. Amen.

In the Courtroom
(JOB 31:35)

JOB 31–33
1 COR. 9:1–18
PSALM 136:1–9

El Shaddai, I have long worshipped You as the almighty God of the universe, but I usually approach You as my Abba Father. If I came before You in court, I would be like Job, puzzled and uncertain. At least he recognized that he was on trial, that he had an accuser, although he didn't know the full story. How I thank You that You included the courtroom scene in Your Word. If Satan comes to accuse me, Your Son stands at Your right hand, speaking on my behalf. You justified me; You'll toss out any complaint placed at my door. Oh Lord, may I live in that freedom—even when I'm under attack. Amen.

Temptation

(1 Corinthians 10:12–13)

Job 34–36
1 Cor. 9:19–10:13
Psalm 136:10–26

*H*eavenly Father, You know how easy it is for me to strut like a peacock, unaware that I'm about to fall into sin. Forgive me. May I keep in mind my own history and the examples of those who have gone before me. The older I get, the more I realize that none of the trials and temptations that come my way are unique. Thank You for the testimonies of those who have overcome similar circumstances, for their support. But mostly I need to depend on You. Even when it feels like I have more than my fair share of problems, You have promised to make a way out or to give me strength to endure. I cling to that hope. Amen.

Glorify God in Everything

(1 Corinthians 10:31)

Job 37–39

1 Cor. 10:14–11:1

Psalm 137

*L*ord God, through the years, churches have created different lists of how Christians should behave. I don't always agree. I'm an American, and I'm prone to claim my rights. Forgive me when I harm my fellow Christians as I claim my freedom. If I am choosing an activity, let me keep Paul's questions in mind: Am I gratifying the flesh, or is it beneficial to myself and others? How will my choice seek the good of others? Oh Lord, I fall so far short in this area. May I live in such a way as to glorify You and to build others up. Amen.

God Answers Job
(JOB 42:1–6)

*O*h Lord God! When I truly encounter You, how I fall in awe and tremble before You. How I thank You for Job's story. He spoke truth, but he had limited knowledge. How I need these reminders that You are God and I am not. As Job says, sometimes I speak of things too wonderful for me. Who am I, a poor woman, to question the hand of my Creator? I am nothing. Every now and then You bring me to a place where I see a glimpse of You, more than I have seen before, and I am humbled before You. As I run to my Abba Father, remind me that You are the sovereign God of the universe and to trust in You. Amen.

Day 248

I Am Known

(PSALM 139:1–6)

ECCLESIASTES 1:1–3:15

1 COR. 12:1–26

PSALM 139:1–6

*C*reator God, You knit me together. But Your involvement doesn't stop at conception. You keep a detailed diary of my comings and goings. You would be the perfect expert witness in a trial, explaining where I was, what I was doing, and why, at any point in time. I can't hide before You. I can't escape. You know the words I'm going to speak before they come out. If I back away, You're there. I can't run away—You're in front of me. You are so big, so powerful, so awesome that I can't understand. And yet You still want to be in a relationship with me. The tiny little insignificant speck that I am. I praise You and thank You! Amen.

Think Before Speaking

ECCL. 3:16–6:12
1 COR. 12:27–13:13
PSALM 139:7–18

When I come to worship, Lord, let me bring listening ears. I am prone to ramble, to say what I think You want to hear. Test me and know my thoughts. You, the God I serve, want an eager learner rather than someone who mindlessly follows rules without seeking the purpose behind them. Keep me from rash promises and, even worse, from making vows. I thank You for Your forgiveness in the past, but keep me from repeating that sin again. Stop me from jumping into things without counting the cost. Forgive me, Lord, when I do. For You know the best course of action always, and when I don't understand, I know Your ways are higher than my ways. Amen.

Transparency
(Psalm 139:23–24)

Ecclesiastes 7:1–9:12

1 Cor. 14:1–22

Psalm 139:19–24

*M*y Lord and Master, I don't want anything to come between us. You know me better than I know myself. Search me, know my heart, reveal me to myself. Roll my anxious thoughts around in the palm of Your hand. Crush the boulders that crush my spirit into sand; blow them away by the breath of Your Spirit. Reveal to me any offensive way. Convict me of sin. Reveal any patterns of behavior that will lead me into harm. Open my eyes to warning signs that I'm headed in the wrong direction. May I follow the straight and narrow path outlined for me; lead me in the way everlasting. Amen.

Orderliness

(1 Corinthians 14:40)

Ecclus. 9:13–12:14
1 Cor. 14:23–15:11
Psalm 140:1–8

Lord Jesus, the head of the church, how sad You must be to see the partitions we carve into it. The divisive, selfish behavior at Corinth deeply disturbed Paul. Today we worship and serve in the culture of fractured churches, denomination fighting denomination. I pray my church will come together in a unity of spirit and broadness of mind. May we reach decisions by prayer and in order, centered on hearing from You and worshipping You as one, not bent on individual preferences. To the extent it's possible, let community churches set minor differences aside to spread the good news to those who haven't heard. Amen.

Day 252

Celebrating Spring
(SONG OF SOLOMON 2:11–13)

SONG 1–4
1 COR. 15:12–34
PSALM 140:9–13

Lord God, how I treasure these beautiful verses about spring—and their association with love. Even in Bible times people's thoughts turned to love as the season changed. No wonder so many couples marry in June. The arrival of spring enlivens my senses. Flowers bloom on trees and bushes, in gardens, and along the ground. Doves coo and songbirds sing as they repeat their mating rituals. The aroma of fruit and flowers and rain fills the air. An explosion of color dispenses with the white of winter. And in all this, we celebrate the promise of eternal life through the resurrection. Thank You, Lord. Amen.

Where Is Death's Sting?

(1 Corinthians 15:55)

Day 253

Song 5–8

1 Cor. 15:35–58

Psalm 141

Oh everlasting God, how glorious. This mortal body won't trap me forever. One day I will be fully restored in body, mind, and spirit. At last, I will be everything You created me to be, inside and out. I will join with all creation to glorify You and enjoy You forever. I don't have to worry about those who have gone before me. They're in heaven waiting for me—the ones I've met, those I never met, and those who will come after me. My eternal life offers so much more than my few years on earth. Let me make the most of my years here, and may I use them to prepare for everlasting life. Thank You! Praise You! Amen.

Day 254

Isaiah 1–2

1 Corinthians 16

Psalm 142

Walking in the Light with the World

(Isaiah 2:1–5)

Mighty God, I read these verses and weep in wonder. Now nations gather in the mountains for the Winter Olympics. I watch the spectacle and imagine the day when people from all the nations of the earth will gather at Your holy mountain to seek You. Speed the day when everyone will want to know and obey Your ways. Hasten that day of peace. Only Your kingdom will bring freedom from war machines. With that bold of a dream, may I boldly walk the streets of my earthly city, a beacon of light to the world around me. Amen.

Comfort

(2 Corinthians 1:1–11)

Isaiah 3–5
2 Cor. 1:1–11
Psalm 143:1–6

Day 255

Wonderful Counselor, I can never thank You enough for Your comfort, given to me so that I may in turn comfort those around me. Open my eyes to those who are in pain. May I never speak of my troubles without testifying to Your loving care. Give me the grace to relieve the sorrow and be transparent so that I may encourage those who are going through their own difficult times, those who are hurting. May Your constant comfort strengthen our feet and spread among Your people. Together, may we be the arms and feet of Your love to the world. Amen.

Isaiah 6–8

2 Cor. 1:12–2:4

Psalm 143:7–12

Burning Coals

(Isaiah 6:6–7)

Lord God, when Your Word speaks of fire, I flinch. Help me to understand how fire plays a role in the life of a believer. Whether Your discipline comes in a fierce firestorm or from the touch of a single live coal, burn away the impurities and make me holy. I thank You for loving me enough to make me all I was created to be in the heat of Your fire. Its touch on my lips may burn for a moment but will not consume me. You refine me to send me with Your message. Set my lips on fire wherever I go. Amen.

A Son Is Born

(Isaiah 9:1–7)

Isaiah 9–10
2 Cor. 2:5–17
Psalm 144

_L_ord God, Your names roll off my tongue as Handel's music resonates in my mind. Wonderful Counselor, Mighty God, Everlasting Father, Prince of Peace. But this passage also reminds me of the transformation Your coming made in my life, the salvation exchange: You replace dishonor with honor, shut out darkness with light, and fill me with life, joy, and freedom from oppression. You have put me under a rule of justice and righteousness. The more I mature in faith, the brighter Your light shines. I'm on my way to the eternal city where You are the light. Amen.

Find Words

(Psalm 145)

Isaiah 11–13

2 Corinthians 3

Psalm 145

My mouth speaks in praise of You, oh Lord. Your wonders fill the accounts of my days. Forgive me when I allow foul talk or speech to cross my lips. When I speak of You, I never run out of news to report, good news to cheer and build people up. You are God my King. No matter how accurate my instruments, how precise my words, I fall short of measuring Your greatness, Your wonder, and Your splendor. Use me in my weakness. May I pass on the stories of Your goodness to others. May Your praise remain constantly in my mouth. Amen.

All Good Gifts
(PSALM 146)

*M*y Lord and God, I am blessed. Whatever happiness, peace, and hope I have comes from You, the great I Am that Abraham and Moses served. How can I be anything but blessed when I can follow in their footsteps? I thank You that my days will unfold exactly as You order them to be. You are the Creator God, and You are forever faithful to Your people. This is why I ask You to uphold the cause of the oppressed and those who suffer, wherever they are. You love the righteous. You love me, and I giggle at the thought. The God who created everything sees me. You know me and love me still. Hallelujah and amen.

Day 260

Isaiah 17–19
2 Corinthians 5
Psalm 147:1–11

Reconciliation
(2 Corinthians 5)

*H*eavenly Father, You have reconciled the world to Yourself in Your Son, Christ, and entrusted that message—more than a message, a ministry—to Your church. May we work for intentional reconciliation. May I speak and live this truth in every way to every person that I meet today. Send ministers of reconciliation, whether missionaries, residents, tourists, businessmen, or others, among people who don't know You. May a passion for reconciliation burn within Christians who encounter those who have rejected You. May Your new life be evident to all, and may they be prepared to give all honor to You. Amen.

Letter of Recommendation

(2 CORINTHIANS 6:3–10)

*L*ord God, when I read Paul's summary of his ministry, I scratch my head. I don't understand the economy of Your kingdom. How is it a commendation to be regarded with dishonor, rejected as imposters? Paul contended that he was willing to be dismissed by the world to bring about the glorious news of Your kingdom. Then I think of people like Martin Luther King Jr. who were willing to be despised for the sake of peace. If great men have suffered for worldly peace, how much more should I risk my reputation and my finances on Your behalf? Not foolishly, but let me not hold back a penny or an ounce of myself worrying about others' opinions of me. Amen.

Two Sides
(Isaiah 24:14–17)

Isaiah 24:1–26:19

2 Corinthians 7

Psalm 148

Lord God, shouts of joy come from the west. The east gives glory to You. The islands rise out of the sea to exalt Your name. Worldwide. You are glorified as the Righteous One. Praise rises to You from sunset to sunset, in waves as the earth whirls through its day. But sometimes those praises are reduced to a whisper in the din of sinful voices, when the darkness of men's hearts inundates my senses. Thank You that Your light breaks that darkness and I hear Your voice because I am Your sheep. May more and more people across the globe join in the song until at last no other sound is heard. Amen.

The Last Psalm

(PSALM 150)

Almighty God, this is such a perfect psalm to end the Bible's hymnbook. May we praise You in Your sanctuary. May our praises echo from the heavens. Let us speak of Your power in action, of Your greatness beyond compare. May our voices, our instruments, our very bodies join together as one, praising You. Let everything on earth, from the rippling waterfall to trees whistling in the wind and rain pounding on the earth, bring glory to Your name. Let everything that has breath—a bee's buzz, a whale's song, an infant's cry—praise You. Amen.

ISAIAH 26:20–28:29
2 CORINTHIANS 8
PSALM 149–150

Day 264

Cheerful Giving
(2 CORINTHIANS 9:6–8)

ISAIAH 29–30

2 CORINTHIANS 9

PROVERBS 1:1–9

*L*ord Jesus, I thank You for people who exemplify cheerful givers, like George Müeller, Albert Schweitzer, and my daughter. Thank You for the joy of giving. Show me where and to whom and what to give. Let me give endlessly of nonmonetary gifts like prayer. But especially help me to give my money cheerfully. Forgive me when I'm stingy. Give me fiscal sense to give wisely. Yet let me not depend on "my" job or "my" bank account to tide me over. You will always make sure I have everything I need for every good work, including generous giving. Amen.

Making My Mind Obey
(2 Corinthians 10:5)

Isaiah 31–33

2 Corinthians 10

Proverbs 1:10–22

*A*ll-wise God, thank You for addressing my doubts in the past. But my intellectual questions are only half of the problem. I fight to bring my thoughts into obedience when emotions and memories from my past attack, trying to take over how I think. The battle continues all day long. Satan wants to plant thoughts that are contrary to Your truth in my mind. Lift me high above the din of the arguments. Give me a voice to shout down falsehoods with sacrifices of praise. May I drown the false accusations and incorrect thoughts by hiding Your Word in my heart. Amen.

The Way of Holiness
(ISAIAH 35)

Isaiah 34–36
2 Corinthians 11
Proverbs 1:23–26

Lord God, You've set me and all Your people on the way of holiness. You strengthen my unfit, arthritic limbs and put on my walking shoes. It's time for me to get into shape. I want to be strong, not fearful, obeying Your command. I can't wait to see the wonders You will perform, both in the spiritual and in the natural realms. I look forward to seeing people with physical disabilities restored to full physical health. I want to travel the new earth after the wastelands of our planet pass away. Thank You for the redeemed who stroll by my side. Your gladness and joy rest on us as we walk hand in hand toward our eternal home. Amen.

Glory in Weakness
(2 Corinthians 12:9–10)

Isaiah 37–38
2 Cor. 12:1–10
Proverbs 1:27–33

*O*mnipotent God, many times I've felt weak in the frailty of my humanity. This is one of those times. Instead of rejecting my weakness, teach me to rejoice because whatever I accomplish will come from You, not myself. There is no better position for me to be in. In this hour, when I own my faint and feeble nature, I also gain strength. For that reason, I will boast about my weaknesses so that any good that comes will point others to You. May I disappear completely, my life a trophy in the showcase of Your grace. Amen.

Day 268

Open for Business
(ISAIAH 40:28–29)

ISAIAH 39–40

2 COR. 12:11–13:14

PROVERBS 2:1–15

*E*ternal, always-faithful God, what a promise You made for the times I feel forgotten or overlooked. You're not a "here today, gone tomorrow" kind of God. You don't say, "See you later," or hang a sign saying OUT TO LUNCH. You don't come and go. You're always open for business 24-7, 365 days a year, and You're always at peak performance. Your care doesn't change based on the time of day, the month or year. You don't need updates. You know all there is to know about everything. What an awesome God I serve! And You share all that energy and power and strength with me. Amen.

Place of No Return
(PROVERBS 2:16–22)

ISAIAH 41–42
GALATIANS 1
PROVERBS 2:16–22

Heavenly Father, I tremble at these words: "Surely [his] house leads down to death" (Proverbs 2:18 NIV). How I thank You for keeping me from sexual impurity. But You know the temptations of my mind. I thank You for the glorious beauty of the marital relationship, for the picture of a man and woman unified in marriage, for its sheer joy. Guard my mind and heart for You, that You will be at the center of any friendship I have with a man. I pray also for others who are married, church leaders, families, and friends: Keep their bond strong. Keep them from falling into adultery, which can lead to death and destruction in marriages and families. Amen.

Isaiah 43:1–44:20

Galatians 2

Proverbs 3:1–12

*H*eavenly Father, I confess my tendency to dwell on the past, on the mistakes I made and the way I hurt myself and those I love. Transform the patterns of my mind. May I put those mistakes behind me, as far as the east is from the west. Open my eyes to the new road You are paving ahead. In the wilderness of life, it springs forth like a well-marked path through the forest. It will lead me from harm to Your good, perfect, pleasing will. May I follow Your lead by the light of Your Word. Amen.

Forever Family
(ISAIAH 45:22–24)

ISAIAH 44:21–46:13
GALATIANS 3:1–18
PROVERBS 3:13–26

Everlasting Father, You never take away Your promises. Your blessings on me today are due in part to a faithful ancestor of mine a thousand years ago. I thank You for that person's faithfulness, whoever they were. I find comfort in knowing You'll show similar favor to my descendants. You'll watch over them and correct them when they go astray. I pray that they'll live faithfully before You. How thankful I am for Your faithfulness. You haven't forgotten that squire in medieval England, that peasant listening to Saint Patrick, or perhaps even a Viking. You will remember all of us and one day return for us. Amen.

Day 272

Refine Me

(ISAIAH 48:10–11)

ISAIAH 47:1–49:13

GALATIANS 3:19–29

PROVERBS 3:27–35

*T*hank You, Lord, for testing and refining me instead of washing Your hands of me. Why did You choose such a fragile vessel? In faith I believe Your choice makes me worthy and capable. Forgive me for shaming You before others. You won't let anything take Your rightful place as Lord of my life. I praise You for Your discipline that comes from Your heart of love. When Your work is finished, I can join others in lifting up Your name above every name. Burn away my sin and impurities, that I may better reflect Your glory. Amen.

Engraving
(ISAIAH 49:18)

ISAIAH 49:14–51:23
GALATIANS 4:1–11
PROVERBS 4:1–19

Lord God, I got to hold my great-granddaughter for the first time yesterday. When her long fingers, short compared to mine, grip my hands, I feel a fierce love for this new person asleep in my arms. I can't imagine forgetting her or failing to do everything possible to help her. So how is it that I doubt, wondering if You have forgotten me? As incredible, as impossible, as it seems, You have engraved me on the palm on Your hands. I am etched on Your heart, Your favorite accessory. May I live and move in that confidence. Amen.

Day 274

Childlessness

(GALATIANS 4:27)

ISAIAH 52–54

GALATIANS 4:12–31

PROVERBS 4:20–27

God of all comfort, there are few things more painful than the empty arms of a woman longing for a child. My arms ache for my daughter who died. I met a woman whose infant only lived for minutes, but we both felt as one. I think of those women who have not yet carried a child to term. For those who are unmarried and celibate, childless. That longing for motherhood can only come from You. But You don't leave us there. You bring us joy for sorrow, fullness for emptiness, an enlarged territory instead of narrow spaces—whether that comes by children or in our relationship with You or through a myriad of other ways. Amen.

Isaiah 55–57
Galatians 5
Proverbs 5:1–14

Father God, I thank You for gathering outsiders to Your holy mountain, that You welcome me to come and worship alongside Your holy people. May the news reach those who haven't received an invitation yet. Make the hearts of those who have rejected You tender. Bombard them with invitations time and time again, until the gathering is complete. I look forward to the day when all may know the God of the nations, the God of justice, salvation, and right. When You call us, may we gladly respond, accepting Your forgiveness and binding ourselves to You in Your great love. Amen.

Day 276

Isaiah 58–59

Galatians 6

Proverbs 5:15–23

Sowing and Reaping
(Galatians 6:7–10)

Lord of the harvest, I thank You for rewarding the faithfulness of those who come to the nursing home where I live, teaching, loving, ministering. You have increased their flock with new people eager to learn and participate. I come back to You, pleading for your workers with willing hearts and hands to join their efforts. I pray that they will continue to sow without growing weary. May I follow their example, and Your command, to do good to all people, especially to believers who live in the nursing home with me. You are faithful, even here. Amen.

The Year of the Lord's Favor
(Isaiah 61)

Isaiah 60–62
Ephesians 1
Proverbs 6:1–5

Sovereign Lord, the greater my trouble—the more contempt hurled at me—the more fervent my prayer. In fact, teach me to shout for joy, because for every godly trouble on earth there's increase and treasure in heaven. It can never be stolen or tarnished. Let all that is in me thank You when times grow dark, because that's where I see Your love and glory most clearly. The year of the Lord's favor—how I thank You that I live on this side of the cross in history. Clothe me in a garment of praise instead of a spirit of despair. Grow my life, branch by branch, until I am a tall oak in the garden of Your splendor. Amen.

ISAIAH 63:1–65:16

EPHESIANS 2

PROVERBS 6:6–19

My Lord and Savior, I have a shameful past like everyone else. There was a time I gave into the cravings of the flesh, with its sinful desires. *But*—that glorious word—You wiped that away. The deed is done. Oh, make Your new life in me evident to all. Free me from that shame. Forgive me when I react in anger born out of past hostilities. Break down the walls I put in place to protect a frightened and helpless child. May I ever reach out from the position of Your peace and Your love and not from my pain. Amen.

One Hope

ISAIAH 65:17–66:24
EPH. 3:1–4:16
PROVERBS 6:20–26

*L*ord God, thank You for the hope I share with all Christians. One body, one Spirit, at birth. You gave me hope when You called me, a hope that I will know the Son of God in all His majesty and fullness and that I'll be unified with other Christians and with You. Let us exercise our gifts to build up one another. Use my gift of encouragement to share that hope, and may I receive what others have to share with me. Teach us not to neglect the times we are to gather together to give and receive. We are so much stronger together than standing alone. Amen.

Speak the Truth in Love

(EPHESIANS 4:22–27)

JEREMIAH 1–2

EPHESIANS 4:17–32

PROVERBS 6:27–35

Lord Jesus, clean my vessel, my being inside and out, today. Wash away the stench of deceitful desires. Fill my mind with a new attitude so that I might pour out new wine, righteous and holy. When something comes up today that frustrates or angers me, let me release it right then. Replace that resentment with insight and compassion for the one who has hurt me. Let me speak truth in love, seeking to build others up and not to tear them down. Make love the constant that quickly smothers sparks of anger. May I learn about trusting others by trusting You. Amen.

Breaking Up the Ground
(JEREMIAH 4:3–4)

*L*ord God, how am I supposed to apply these verses? Am I to break up the sins in my heart into tiny pieces? If people could do that on their own, Jesus wouldn't have had to die. Maybe it's more like Hebrews 12, where I'm told to remove everything that distracts me and leads me to sin. Or maybe You want to soften the hardness of my heart so that I may choose to believe and live. You're there, rooting for me, but You don't decide for me. May I use the rake of Your Word to crisscross the soil of my heart, digging up hidden thorns and rocks, so that I can produce a more fruitful crop. Amen.

Children and Parents

(Ephesians 6:1–3)

*H*eavenly Father, before all societies and government came into being, You instituted the family— husband, wife, children. It's meant to be one of Your best gifts to us, but too often things go wrong. I no longer have a husband or small children, but I pray for those who do, starting with my own son. May their offspring obey their parents as children and honor them as adults. I pray for fathers, that they won't infuriate their children but teach them gently, training them in Your ways. Although Paul only mentions fathers, I pray the same things for mothers. May homes be filled with Your love, and not anger or abuse. Amen.

Paul's Prayer for the Philippians
(PHILIPPIANS 1:4–11)

Day 283

JEREMIAH 6:1–7:26
PHILIPPIANS 1:1–26
PROVERBS 8:1–11

*L*ord Jesus, what comfort I take in Paul's confidence. You began the good work in me, and You will finish it when I see You. I would certainly fail on my own. And between now and then, I ask that my love will abound both in wisdom and in depth of insight. May I gain not only head knowledge but also understanding. May I put Your principles into practice. I pray the same for others who believe in You. Lead us into purity, blamelessness, and holiness. May all that knowledge permeate our lives, increasing the crop of righteousness to the glory and praise of God. Amen.

Spiritual MRSA

(Jeremiah 8:20–22)

Jer. 7:27–9:16

Philippians 1:27–2:18

Proverbs 8:12–21

*L*ord, how foolish the Israelites were, to seek peace at any price instead of going to You to cure their incurable wound. How foolish I am at times, when I reject Your good and perfect will and instead look for healing elsewhere. I keep holding out a palm branch, seeking allies, but my choices have turned the ground beneath my feet into quicksand. Forgive me. Turn my heart to You. Open my eyes to Your commands. Instead of seeking help elsewhere, may I turn to my balm in Gilead. Let me meditate on Your precepts. Show me how to put them into practice. May I commit them to memory, that they will spring to mind when I am tempted to go in the wrong direction. I want to be a faithful resident in Your kingdom. Amen.

Reasons to Boast

Jer. 9:17–11:17
Philippians 2:19–30
Proverbs 8:22–36

*L*ord God Almighty, it's okay to boast, but I have to carefully consider what's worth shouting about. If I think I'm smart, wise, strong, or rich—even if it's true—those attributes don't come from me. They are from You, Your good gifts. I struggle with how to share my good news without feeling like I'm bragging. But may I gladly share what You've taught me about Yourself. I have learned a small part of who You are. Your kindness, justice, and righteousness dictate all You do. That's how I live and thrive. They are Your delight; make them my joy and my boast. Amen.

Day 286

JER. 11:18–13:27

PHILIPPIANS 3

PROVERBS 9:1–6

Wisdom's Pillars

(PROVERBS 9:1–6)

*L*ord God, I'm standing in the house with wisdom's pillars and I'm not sure what I'm looking at. She encourages me to seek insight rather than to live according to what makes sense in my own eyes. You don't want me to ask for wisdom from my acquaintances. Your Word is the banquet You have spread open for me. Each bite increases my insight; each taste presents new truth. You have so very much to teach me. I can never eat too much, and there is a continual supply. This is where I should come to feast. Amen.

Peace in Chaos
(Philippians 4:7)

JEREMIAH 14–15
PHILIPPIANS 4
PROVERBS 9:7–18

*P*rince of Peace, You know how interruptions disturb my serenity. I like things in the order I prefer. How often that fails to happen. Guard my heart and mind with Your peace. May I rest and wait in quiet, whether the hour is early or late, whether I am longing for the arrival of sleep or bemoaning the lack of promised human help. May I remain happy and content, calm and not flustered when prolonged delay becomes a flurry of activity. Have I made time my god? Forgive me. Let me not allow time to be my taskmaster, but my slave to put to work for You. Amen.

Day 288

A Deceitful Heart

(JEREMIAH 17:7–10)

JEREMIAH 16–17
COLOSSIANS 1:1–23
PROVERBS 10:1–5

*L*ord God, these words simultaneously offer hope and fear. If I trust in You, I am blessed. But when You search my heart, will You find deceit? Do I say I trust You but instead rely on what I can see and touch? Am I underhanded with You, claiming to follow You while going my own way? Forgive me. Thank You for replacing my incurable heart with the new one given to me at salvation, that I may serve You with all that I am. Only when I place 100 percent of my confidence in You will You plant me like a tree by streams of water. Only Your pure water will produce constant, unhindered growth. Amen.

Stirring Up Conflict

(Proverbs 10:12)

*L*ord God, I'd rather skip this verse. I hate conflict, my part in it, how my stomach churns and I wince at the approach of my opponent. How easily I go from resolving differences to sinning against my fellow man and You. If hatred stirs up conflict, then it starts in my mind and heart. I feel like I've been wronged, and often I have valid reasons. But You expect better of me. You invite me to cover other people's offenses with love instead of responding with hate. You provided the perfect example. Make me like You. Where there is hatred, let me sow love. Amen.

Day 290

JER. 20:7–22:19

COLOSSIANS 2:16–3:4

PROVERBS 10:15–26

Depression

(JEREMIAH 20:14–18)

*M*y loving Father, I thank You that Jeremiah's deep emotions are included in Your Word, as painful as they are. How apt I am to think that when I'm depressed, I must be doing something wrong. That You can't use me until I get over it. Here's the example of a prophet, the one You used to confront Judah during the final years of her downward spiral. How much truth would be lost to the world without his book of prophecy? And yet he felt worthless. Like You did for Jeremiah, do also for me: keep me going even when I don't feel it in my heart. You are always able, even when I wish I were someone, anyone, else. Amen.

A New Wardrobe

(COLOSSIANS 3:12–13)

JER. 22:20–23:40
COLOSSIANS 3:5–4:1
PROVERBS 10:27–32

*L*ord God, the next time I go shopping for new clothes, let me remember this list from Paul. May I be more concerned about expanding my spiritual wardrobe to accommodate my new self than purchasing new outfits for my body. May I choose compassion, kindness, humility, gentleness, and patience as staples. None of those come naturally to me, Lord, but they are mine because You are in me. Add Your love and forgiveness as the necessary accessories that will bind the church together in unity. Choose my clothing and dress me in kingdom fashions. Amen.

Day 292

Jeremiah 24–25
Colossians 4:2–18
Proverbs 11:1–11

Sent Away for My Own Good
(Jeremiah 24:4–7)

Lord, did men like Daniel, Ezekiel, and Mordecai realize they had been sent away from Israel for their good? You protected them from the desolation of Judah's final days and kept them from annihilation. You sent them to a place where they would prosper and to a king who was sympathetic to their faith. There, and back in Israel, You wanted to build them up and give them hearts to know You. Maybe that's why You turned me aside from the plans I believed You had for me and led me elsewhere, to my place of exile. Here You have prospered me and given me friends and a ministry I never expected. Thank You. Amen.

JEREMIAH 26–27
1 THES. 1:1–2:8
PROVERBS 11:12–21

God my Father, what do people think of when my name comes to mind? Oh, to have a testimony such as the church at Thessalonica had. May others remember my work produced by faith. May any good I do, any words I write, speak of You and all You have done and not of me and all I have done. May my labor be prompted, not by duty or selfishness, but by Your love flowing through me. When I am called to endure—which in a sense is every day until I get to heaven—may hope inspire me. In work, in labor, in endurance, keep my eye on the prize of living in You. Amen.

Day 294

Finding God

(JEREMIAH 29:11–13)

JEREMIAH 28–29
1 THES. 2:9–3:13
PROVERBS 11:22–26

*L*ord God, You want to be found. If I seek Your face with all my heart, I will find You. It's like following a maze and catching glimpses of You each step of the way. Each one shows me more. Even when I'm in heaven, where You are the light and I am worshipping before Your throne, I'll rejoice in spending eternity coming to know You in all Your fullness. Because I have seen You only in part, I only comprehend a small portion of Your plan. You say You have given me new hope and a future. I accept Your promise by faith. I thank You for what I have already seen of You. Amen.

Saving Lives
(PROVERBS 11:30)

JER. 30:1–31:22
1 THES. 4:1–5:11
PROVERBS 11:27–31

*H*eavenly Father, what a foolish, self-serving person I can be. I rejoice that I am a living tree growing by the stream, for the fruit that grows on my branches. And I do rejoice in the fruit You give me—abundant fruit with a heavenly flavor that can only come from You. But that fruit isn't meant for me alone. You give it to me to share. If I'm planted by Your stream, if I'm wise in how I prune and fertilize, through me You'll save lives. I'll minister to here-and-now needs. I'll also point the lost to You, their Savior. Give me the wisdom to know how You want me to reach out. Amen.

A Timeless Covenant
(JEREMIAH 31:31–36)

JER. 31:23–32:35
1 THES. 5:12–28
PROVERBS 12:1–14

Everlasting Father and Prince of Peace, oh, what a joy to read the promise and know I received a new covenant in Your Son. You have remade me, a dwelling place for Your Spirit. I don't have to ask someone else to explain it, because You make it clear. I'm also in covenant with Your people, the community of believers, yet Your plan for me doesn't rest on what happens to my spouse, child, or neighbor. You have placed Your will in my mind that I may remember it and written it on my heart that I may obey. While my body will one day crumble into dust, Your covenant with me will remain strong and unbreakable. Amen.

It's a God Thing
(JEREMIAH 33:6–9)

*L*ord God, no wonder You told Jeremiah that You were doing wonderful things in answer to his prayer. Like me, his petitions focused on his needs. You answered his prayer with tremendous promises. You would bring the Jews back to the land, to prosper them, if only they would obey You. You offered to restore, heal, and rebuild with peace, security, and forgiveness. But all those things had a single purpose: to glorify You. The transformation brought You not only praise and honor, but also renown and joy. It caused people from across the globe to seek You. You share the joy of restoring the praise of human voices with me. Lord, whatever good happens to me, let me turn it back to You. Amen.

Peace at All Times

(2 THESSALONIANS 3:16)

JER. 34:8–36:10

2 THESSALONIANS 3

PROVERBS 12:21–28

*L*ord of lords and Prince of Peace, I pray You will spread Your peace at all times and in every way. I want a perfect personal peace, but I pray even more for my community of faith. You are with all of us. Your grace lies on us. You are unchangeable. So how is it we find so much to disagree about? Let me seek that peace for myself and for others. Let us make harmony our goal daily, especially in times of potential strife and even when the battle rages. May You give wholeness to us in every way, free from war and disturbance. Amen.

Pursuing Good or Bad
(Proverbs 13:2–3)

Lord God, I'm gaining a greater appreciation for Solomon's commonsense couplets. He packs in so much! And he doesn't always make the obvious connection. In today's passage, he doesn't say the opposite of good things is the lack of them. Instead, he expresses the results of unrighteousness: the unfaithful have an appetite for violence. How ugly. My heart's desires, left unchecked, will lead me to selfish, demanding, angry thoughts that tend toward violence in what I say and do. Rather, teach me to be wise, to seek righteousness, to protect my lips, that I may preserve life and not destroy it. Replace any angry thoughts within me with Your love and peace. Amen.

Day 300

Then There's Pride

(PROVERBS 13:10)

JER. 38:14–40:6

1 TIMOTHY 1:18–3:13

PROVERBS 13:5–13

Wonderful Counselor, You know how I've struggled my whole life with wanting to be proven right. I've never thought of that as pride, but it certainly leads to strife. Forgive me. I thank You for the maturity to accept others' theological and ideological beliefs. Teach me that same wisdom in my daily life, especially in the circumstances I live in. May I listen more than I speak, that I may learn from the wisdom of others. Make me more eager to gather wisdom than to spread it, for my wisdom is no wisdom at all unless it comes from You. If I boast, let it be that I know You, the One true God. Amen.

In Training

(1 TIMOTHY 4:6–10)

JER. 40:7–42:22

1 TIM. 3:14–4:10

PROVERBS 13:14–21

*L*ord Jesus, what a difference in priorities between what Paul advocates and what we hear today. Physical regimens? Useful but not as important as godliness. Seeking God offers profit in every area of my life, including the physical, both in this world and the next. It's a good investment—give me the eyes to see what a blessing it is. Keep me from being sidetracked by myths and old wives' tales. Fill my mind with Your truth. If my life isn't godly, if it doesn't measure up to what I say, then no one will listen to my words. Because of my hope in You, I labor and strive toward godliness. Amen.

Day 302

How to Love My Children

(Proverbs 13:22)

Jeremiah 43–44

1 Tim. 4:11–5:16

Proverbs 13:22–25

Heavenly Father, the One who also cares for us like a mother, how I thank You for Your parenting guidance. My children are grown, but there never comes a time when I stop being a mother, in the unique role that grandparents play. What better incentive to pursue righteousness than to know it will bless my grandchildren? Let me be thoughtful about what kind of riches I am storing away for them to receive and to remember me by. Let me set a good example of faith, love, and life. If they follow in my footsteps, may they follow You. Amen.

Escaping with My Life
(JEREMIAH 45:5)

JEREMIAH 45–47
1 TIM. 5:17–6:21
PROVERBS 14:1–6

*H*eavenly Father, it sounds like Baruch dreamed of great things. I know I do. I want a comfortable life, with my physical needs met. I long to see the work I do for the kingdom reach a large number of people, and so I fail to see the individuals in the crowd. Humble me; teach me to be satisfied with the small things. Let me not expect to escape disaster when it falls on the city where I live, the place where I work, on my nation. I thank You that in the worst circumstances, You promise to deliver me. I will survive. How foolish I am to want more when I see people falling on every side. Amen.

Second-Generation Christians

(2 Timothy 1:3–8)

Jer. 48:1–49:6

2 Timothy 1

Proverbs 14:7–22

Lord Jesus, I'm so thankful that the faith I received from my mother now burns brightly in my son. How Lois and Eunice must have rejoiced in Timothy. As beautiful as the legacy of faith in a family is, that flame is different for someone who is the first in their family to be saved. Forgive me when I allow other things, like timidity and fear, to smother the flame and the gifts You want to light with it. When I allow insecurity to hold me back, fill me with power, love, and self-discipline. Let me jump at the chance to share the Gospel. Amen.

Starting Over

(Jeremiah 50:4–5)

Jer. 49:7–50:16
2 Timothy 2
Proverbs 14:23–27

*O*h Lord my Guide, I come to You, seeking You, sadness in my heart for the neglected days, thankful for fresh health and alertness. Thank You for renewing Your covenant with me, not because You had forgotten it, but because I had forgotten You. I kneel before You, acknowledging Your gracious provision, confessing my sin, asking You to cleanse and renew me. May I not go astray, but instead seek Your guidance at every twist in the road ahead. Forgive me when I do stray and bring me back. Thank You for Your eternal embrace. Amen.

Day 306

Small Stuff
(PROVERBS 14:29)

JER. 50:17–51:14

2 TIMOTHY 3

PROVERBS 14:28–35

*O*h Lord, I need this one today. Make me as slow to anger as You are, that I may mine the ores of Your understanding and compassion. How can I claim to know You and Your Word if I lose my patience easily? It makes me think of the saying "Don't fret the small stuff, and it's all small stuff." Compared to the grandeur of Your plan, and with the understanding that nothing happens to me without Your knowledge, I can accept what is, showing patience, waiting for You to fulfill Your will. Keep me from folly, and let me trust in You. Amen.

The Two-Sided Tongue
(Proverbs 15:1–7)

God who spoke the world into being, You have given great power to the tongue. Forgive me when I abuse that power. Cleanse and renew me when I stir up anger and crush spirits with harsh words. Correct my foolish speaking. In its place give me a gentle spirit to respond to anger. May I relay Your wisdom and not my own folly. Let my speech soothe the spirits of those in despair, offering the shade of the tree of life. May I speak of what is upright and true and know when to be silent. Amen.

It's Not Worth It

(Proverbs 15:16–18)

Jer. 52–Lam. 1

Titus 1:1–9

Proverbs 15:10–18

*L*ord God, once again You're reminding me that conflict isn't the best answer, and it's often the last choice to consider. You know my struggles. Perhaps that's why You give me so many opportunities to change and grow, that I will be calm in the face of conflict. Use me to calm troubled people instead of stirring up strife. Oh, make it so. I also pray for those nearest and dearest to me, that I will eat that plate of food I don't like rather than create a fuss. Keep me from allowing momentary problems to fester and grow into a hate-filled boil. Lance me with Your Spirit. Amen.

Wives and Mothers
(Titus 2:4–5)

Lam. 2:1–3:38
Titus 1:10–2:15
Proverbs 15:19–26

God who created families, I pray for young mothers and wives. May their love for their husbands and children burn fiercely and in purity. Make them sensible in their management and modest in their dress, thoughts, and behavior. May they work hard at home and on the job. Teach them to be kind to friends, neighbors, and strangers. I lift up those wives whose husbands aren't believers, that they will know how to both honor their husbands and obey You, especially when their husbands' wills contradict Yours. I pray for their spouses' salvation and that unity will rule in their hearts. Amen.

You Answered My Call

(LAMENTATIONS 3:55–58)

LAM. 3:39–5:22
TITUS 3
PROVERBS 15:27–33

*L*ord God, when I tumble to the bottom of a pit, like the Jews who were taken into captivity, I'm weary in mind, body, and spirit. I am too crushed to utter any prayer beyond my cry for help. Oh, the wonder of the Holy Spirit, who takes that wordless prayer and intercedes for me. Like the father of the prodigal son who actively looked for his son's return, You actively await my pleas. You run to me and assuage my fears. You take up my case, redeem me, and change me. You prepare me for a better quality life—the life I was designed for, eternal life. Praise the Lord. Amen and amen.

No Longer a Slave

(PHILEMON 1:14–17)

EZEKIEL 1:1–3:21
PHILEMON
PROVERBS 16:1–9

*L*ord and Master, to whom I owe my service, Onesimus's story makes me think about the continuing racial strife because of the legacy of slavery. I don't understand, can't understand, what it's like to be black in America today, because my skin is white. I can imagine how hard it was for Onesimus to return to the situation he'd fled, uncertain of his reception. Like Onesimus and Philemon, many of us who were once on the outside are now brothers and sisters in Christ. Let our oneness in You be a new beginning, Your Son's blood the thing that binds us together. We are forever family. Let us stand up for one another. May churches take the lead in healing the racial divide. Amen.

Working Things Out

(PROVERBS 16:20)

EZEKIEL 3:22–5:17
HEBREWS 1:1–2:4
PROVERBS 16:10–21

Eternal, wise God, I boast that everything will work out when Your Word permeates my life, when I live according to Your revealed will. If I use the Bible as a handbook for my business and personal affairs, I will enjoy a good, if not wealthy, life. The better I understand Your Word, the greater the chances my efforts will succeed. The more I study, the greater my skill set. When I turn to Your Word, I don't have to anticipate the future. You've already paved the way before me. Past experience has demonstrated the truth of Your Word. Its pages fill my mind and mouth with wisdom. Thank You! Amen.

Crown of Glory

EZEKIEL 6–7
HEBREWS 2:5–18
PROVERBS 16:22–33

God Almighty, my gray and hoary head grows more glorious by the day, as gray gives way to white. If those snowy locks testify to a God-loyal life, make every one of them bright and as stain-free as the righteousness You have given to me. Since I live in a culture that doesn't treasure our elders, I thank You for this reminder of how You see me. May I treat my fellow senior saints with honor and dignity. May I see Your beauty in their clouded eyes and gnarled hands. May I accept my long life, and the limitations age brings, as a mark of distinction, bestowed upon me by You. Amen.

Day 314

EZEKIEL 8–10
HEBREWS 3:1–4:3
PROVERBS 17:1–5

Housecleaning

(HEBREWS 3:13)

*G*racious, holy Lord, I come to these chapters in Hebrews with fear and trembling. I confess I don't understand what hardening of the heart means for the Christian and what the consequences are. Such things are too wonderful for me. I pray that instead of hardening, believers in danger will be built up. When I see a brother or sister who is struggling, may I offer my support and prayers. May I not overlook my pesky sins. Forgive me for what I overlook. Sweep the house of my heart clean; dig up any moldy sin that wants to take root. Fill my mind with Your Word and Spirit, that I might not be deceived. Amen.

Keeping My Mouth Shut
(Proverbs 17:9)

Day 315

Ezekiel 11–12

Hebrews 4:4–5:10

Proverbs 17:6–12

*L*oving God, You speak to me in truth and love. You deal with me directly. You don't whisper bad things about me in the ears of others. Oh, that I would be like You! Oh, that You will burn away the disease of my forked tongue, which speaks love with one side and gossips with the other. Sew it back together by Your Holy Spirit; heal it with the ointment of Your *agape* love that will cover a multitude of sins. Forgive me when I repeat that which is best kept secret, and give me the wisdom to know the difference. Amen.

EZEKIEL 13–14

HEB. 5:11–6:20

PROVERBS 17:13–22

My Lifeline

(HEBREWS 6:18–19)

My Lifeline and my promised Hope, I have run to You for my life. I hold on to the sure hope of that sanctuary as my lifeline. I cling to it with everything I have, trusting in nothing and no one else. It guides me past appearances and takes me to Your presence. I hold on with both hands, not letting go to reach for passing fads. Up ahead of me I see Jesus, who has gone before me. May I follow the trail He has blazed. Prepare me to breathe in Your rarefied spiritual air. Amen.

Perfect Fit

(Hebrews 7:25–27)

*L*ord and Savior, I live in a one-size-fits-all world that meets most of my needs but doesn't cater to me. The solutions offered for my problems come with no guarantee of success. Praise to You that Your sacrifice on the cross was a perfect cover for every sin. There are no sins that are excluded (except for the unforgiveable sin, and I'll ask You about that another time). There is no small print. No limitations on how many or which people may come. There is abundant grace, and exactly enough, for everyone born among men. I praise You that You are absolutely, eternally perfect. Amen.

Cedars
(Ezekiel 17:22–23)

Ezek. 16:44–17:24
Hebrews 8:1–9:10
Proverbs 18:1–7

*L*iving Lord, You are a splendid cedar, a life-giving vine, the tree that provides shade everywhere on earth. Your chosen people were branches on that tree, and now You have grafted me in, giving me a new identity I don't deserve. Thank You for the tree that allows me to nest, to rest and multiply, a concert hall where we raise songs of praise. I want to eat Your fruit and drink Your water, both for myself and to offer it to others. Prune me, that I will bear fruit. Use me to spread the seeds of Your life to others, that they may also come to You. Amen.

She Will Surely Live

(EZEKIEL 18:5–9)

Day 319

Ezekiel 18–19
Hebrews 9:11–28
Proverbs 18:8–17

Living God of truth, is this a promise or a description? Pondering it again, I'm struck that You've given me a definition of what real life is. You don't prescribe a trade for extra years but instead paint a portrait of a good, full life. You want me to treat others well, to work at relationships. A good life involves abstaining from instant gratification through things like food or irresponsible spending. You offer me the true life today, if I want it. May Your righteousness in me cause me to seek after what is just and right. Amen.

Day 320

Friends

(Proverbs 18:24)

Ezekiel 20

Hebrews 10:1–25

Proverbs 18:18–24

*H*eavenly Father, sometimes I would rather live without the nuisance of pesky people, the kind of undesirable friends that Solomon wrote about. But You have made me for community. You placed me in my family unit, through the wonderful years as the middle of a three-generation sandwich and now as the elder of the clan. You've also given me all believers as my brothers and sisters. But perhaps the ones I appreciate the most are those who choose me as a friend. I can't thank You enough for all we have meant to each other. I pray for those who don't have much support. Bring someone alongside them, and shelter them within a loving community. Amen.

Holding On

EZEKIEL 21–22
HEBREWS 10:26–39
PROVERBS 19:1–8

*A*uthor and Finisher of my faith, I have confidence knowing that You'll bring my faith race to completion in Christ. But that doesn't mean my steps today come easily or that I never question the cost or doubt the outcome. Replace my questions with acceptance. Overcome my doubt with patience so that I might persevere until the finish line. Give me the endurance to walk when I can't run, to crawl when I can't walk. Prod me to my feet and move me forward when I've fallen. Make me dogged in following Your will. How sweet the day will be when I receive Your promise. Amen.

Day 322

Proof

(Hebrews 11:1)

EZEKIEL 23

HEBREWS 11:1–31

PROVERBS 19:9–14

Unseen God, thank You for the gift of faith, for it is a gift. I don't know why I see You clearly when people I admire deny Your existence for lack of empirical evidence. I thank You for sight and pray for them. In the classroom, faith enables me to comprehend as fact what I can't see or touch. In the courtroom, it's the proof that determines the verdict. Faith is both the confirmation of what I've received from You and the title deed to my inheritance. It gives substance to my spiritual diet. Thank You for the gift of faith that enables me to live in light of Your reality. Amen.

Man Proposes but God Disposes
(Proverbs 19:21)

Day 323

Ezekiel 24–26
Hebrews 11:32–40
Prov. 19:15–21

Sovereign Lord, I love to make plans. I lay out the hours of my days. In my work, I count the cost before I commit to a project. Daily, I discipline myself to accomplish predetermined goals. Then there are the times You step in. You hand me a new assignment. Illness creeps in, and I must turn to You for wisdom and strength in completing my assignment. You turn my small things into big things and my big things into small ones. I seek to make wise use of time, but You operate the stopwatch, reminding me to trust You with my seconds and minutes. Amen.

The Christian Race
(HEBREWS 12:1–2)

EZEKIEL 27–28
HEBREWS 12:1–13
PROVERBS 19:22–29

Wonderful Counselor and Coach, strip me of everything that hinders my race. Author and Finisher of the race, lead me in Jesus' steps and be the wind at my back until I reach the finish line. Thank You for burning away the hindrances and impurities that keep me from running straight for the prize. I trust the transformation process to You as I hide under the shelter of Your wings. You are the instigator of the race and its Reward. You're also the pattern for how to run. If I don't know what steps to take in training, I only need to turn to Your example. Amen.

Bitterness

Day 325

EZEKIEL 29–30
HEBREWS 12:14–29
PROVERBS 20:1–18

Lord God, woe is me! When I look at myself in the mirror of this scripture, I see how ugly I am, what awful things I've done. So often I'm tempted to bitterness, resentful of all the things I would change about my life if I could. So often I'm known as a complainer instead of someone who builds others up. Praise You, I'm changing, but I cringe to think of all the people my negative attitude may have pushed away from You. Forgive me! As Saint Francis said, "Make me an instrument of Your peace. Where there has been hatred, let me sow love." Amen.

Day 326

Sacrifice of Praise
(Hebrews 13)

EZEKIEL 31–32
HEBREWS 13
PROVERBS 20:19–24

Lord God, every minute of the rest of my life, teach me the delightful sacrifice of praise—even on days like today, when I feel out of sorts and fear things will never improve. May Your peace, love, and hope take the place of all those concerns. I praise You because nothing happens to me without Your permission. Everything that I experience works together for Your glory, if not my idea of comfort. With that in mind, may I sing of Your praises in the assembly. Together with Your children, may we shout hallelujahs to our Lord and Savior, Jesus Christ. May the canyons of my despair echo my whispered affirmations of Your love, until they grow stronger and more powerful with each passing day. Amen.

Speaking for an Audience
(EZEKIEL 33:30)

Day 327

EZEK. 33:1–34:10
JAMES 1
PROVERBS 20:25–30

*L*ord God, when I speak of Your love and grace, do people listen to me with genuine interest or for entertainment? How encouraged Ezekiel must have felt when people came by his house, eager to hear from You. In turn, how disheartened he must have been when they didn't act on Your messages to them. They appreciated the performance but rejected the reality. Oh Lord, your prophets have been maligned from of old. Onlookers will do the same to me. Let me not speak to garner praise from men, but because You have called me. When I feel the sting of public disapproval, let me draw closer to You. Amen.

Rock-Bottom Truth

(JAMES 2)

EZEK. 34:11–36:15

JAMES 2

PROVERBS 21:1–8

Heavenly Father, this chapter jumps out with a commonsense approach to faith. My actions speak louder than my words. When I make an unkind comment, it takes a hundred uplifting words to erase the unkind statement. How I act should match what I say, and both speech and actions should be consistent. May people see Your presence in me before I open my mouth. May I not say one thing today and a different thing tomorrow. When I pray about a problem, may I respond to the need if I'm able to do so. Amen.

Reunited

Ezek. 36:16–37:28
James 3
Proverbs 21:9–18

Lord God, how often I regret the divisions within the church, the walls we put up between us. Though You created one of the first schisms when You split Israel into two nations, You never intended for them to remain separated forever. During the exile, You promised to bring both nations back, to establish them in the land under one Shepherd. Your body, the church, also has one Shepherd. One faith, one Lord, one baptism. If today we work with barriers between us, may the day come when those partitions disappear. You prayed that we would be one in love. Keep us from tearing one another down in hate. Amen.

Wrong Desires
(JAMES 4:1–3)

*M*y Lord and Father, these verses bring me to my knees, asking You to change my "wanter" to bring my desires in line with Your will. When I want something so badly—simply to satisfy my whims—I invite all kinds of disaster. I'm led to covet others' possessions. Coveting turns into quarrelling and fighting and murderous hatred. What could have been mine by asking has become a root of evil, something I will not receive because I ask amiss. Forgive me when I make the object of my desire more important than You or others. Keep me clear from such covetousness. Amen.

When to Pray
(JAMES 5:13–18)

EZEKIEL 40
JAMES 5:7–20
PROV. 21:25–31

*L*ord Jesus, how James's words strike at the heart of prayer. Am I in trouble? Pray. Am I happy? Pray. Am I sick? Pray. There isn't a single situation where prayer isn't appropriate. And as I pray, I become aware of the connection between physical and spiritual wholeness. I don't pray in a vacuum. I am to intercede with and for others. In those prayers I will find healing and forgiveness. What a promise! My prayer can be powerful and effective, like Elijah's, who shut the heavens from raining for three years. I hover between pride and awe at that statement, but as Your answers come, may I return all glory to You. Amen.

Wayward Children
(PROVERBS 22:6)

EZEK. 41:1–43:12

1 PETER 1:1–12

PROVERBS 22:1–9

Heavenly Father, I lift up this verse on behalf of parents everywhere whose children have wandered from You, starting with my own family. For my grandchildren growing into adulthood, I pray that they will choose the way they were trained. I pray for parents with young children. May they teach Your eternal truth, with understanding of each child's unique gifts and personality. May they not only teach the rules, but also about how to make choices so that their children will have the skills they need to make the right choices. Let them impart not a set of regulations, but a way of life. Amen.

Spiritual Dialysis
(1 Peter 2:1–3)

EZEK. 43:13–44:31
1 PETER 1:13–2:3
PROVERBS 22:10–23

*L*ord Jesus, I come to You in my unkempt state, my life wrinkled by sinful habits and bad choices, badly in need of a cleansing of my spiritual lifeblood. I thank You for Your forgiveness, instantaneous and irrevocable, when I confess my sins and ask for Your cleansing. I'm asking You to replace ungodly desires with the new. In Your dialysis machine, spin out the past of malice, deceit, hypocrisy, envy, slander. Refill those veins with the milk of Your Word, pure, life sustaining—all I need to grow in You. Let me come to You continuously, seeking to keep my spirit cleansed of the past, that my arteries may remain open and clear. Amen.

Day 334

Make Me a Testimony

(1 PETER 2:12–15)

EZEKIEL 45–46

1 PETER 2:4–17

PROVERBS 22:24–29

*D*ear Lord and Savior, what a daring prayer, to offer my life as a testimony to those who don't know You. May people see evidence in my life of Your ever-reaching and limitless love. May I reveal the truth of Your goodness and seek the good of all without favoritism. Cleanse me; polish the glass of my life, that others may glorify You. Not because of me, but because of You in me. Let me submit to Your authority first and to their benefit next, and not use my freedom to mar my testimony. Amen.

Don't Bother the Fool
(PROVERBS 23:9)

EZEKIEL 47–48
1 PETER 2:18–3:7
PROVERBS 23:1–9

*L*ord God, hear my plea for discernment. Not everyone will listen to me or heed what I say, whether I'm asking for help or offering advice. Foolish me, when I continue to bang my head against the wall. Give me discernment to differentiate between who will listen and who won't. Perhaps I am trying to take Your place in speaking. Other messengers may reach those who don't listen to me. Keep me from becoming defensive. Let me speak only when moved by You. May I accept words of wisdom when they are spoken to me and not reject them. Amen.

Day 336

Praying in a Pickle
(DANIEL 2:17–23)

DANIEL 1:1–2:23
1 PETER 3:8–4:19
PROVERBS 23:10–16

Great God of the heavens, You are the answer to every prayer, the "yes" to our every need. Daniel and his friends pleaded for their lives, and You answered. Was this the first time they received an interpretation of dreams? When I receive such clarity, may I, like Daniel, recognize You as the source of the wisdom and the power behind it. Give me the discernment to know when I have heard from You. I trust You for grace when the message is one I don't want to hear or share. I thank You for the example of Daniel's courage to speak Your truth before the king. Amen.

Even If

Lord God, my heart thrills as I read of Shadrach, Meshach, and Abednego's faith, and I pray mine will mirror theirs. They staked their lives on their trust that You would deliver them from the furnace, and the subsequent miracle proved them right. What I treasure is their unwavering commitment to die by the flame—should You choose not to act—rather than worship the idol of gold set up by man and no real god at all. Whatever block is thrust in my way, may I, like them, refuse to give in to fear of man but boldly serve You, even to death. Amen.

Everything I Need
(2 Peter 1:3–8)

DANIEL 4

2 PETER 1

PROVERBS 23:26–35

*H*eavenly Lord, You have given me everything I need, and not only in the sense of my daily bread. You call me to godliness, which I can't do on my own. You have already equipped me for transformation through my knowledge of You, calling me to Your glory and goodness. Let me grab hold by building on the foundation of faith a seven-layer-strong structure to make me like You: goodness, knowledge, self-control, perseverance, godliness, mutual affection, love. May I continue to grow in all these areas until at last I am home with You. Amen.

Daniel 5

2 Peter 2

Proverbs 24:1–18

Lord God, I need Your glasses to see others clearly. I'm nearsighted when it comes to seeing their needs. They may be struggling to the point of death, and yet I haven't noticed their pain. At other times, I'm farsighted when I envy the good fortune of the righteous. Just as bad is when I rejoice in the misfortune of my enemies. May I look to others to look for ways to help, but let me focus on living a sober, God-pleasing life. May I consider the weight of my deeds in Your scales and overlook that of others. Amen.

The Price of Prayer

(DANIEL 6:1–13)

DANIEL 6:1–7:14

2 PETER 3

PROVERBS 24:19–27

God, to have the testimony of Daniel, that the only thing people fault me for is my prayer life. Oh, to have his courage, that he didn't alter his routine when the law said prayer was an offense against his king. I ponder how prayer triggered not only his problem but also the solution, when he turned to You for help in the den of lions. When have I ever been asked to pay a price for prayer? I thank You that I live in a country that practices religious freedom. There are many who suffer persecution, who must pray in secret. I ask that their courage will match Daniel's and that You will protect them if they are brought to trial. Amen.

The Rule of Love
(1 JOHN 1:7–2:17)

DANIEL 7:15–8:27
1 JOHN 1:1–2:17
PROVERBS 24:28–34

Lord God, may Your Spirit shine Your light on the world around me. May I have the wisdom to discern when my thanksgiving for Your gifts turns into valuing the gift over the Giver. Show me when lust for more things and pride in what I have take Your place on my heart's throne. May I love people, not things. May I love them as You do, giving of myself, placing their needs ahead of my own. May my love point them to You. When I fail, forgive me. I rest in the assurance that You will pardon my sins when I confess them. Let me walk in Your light and love. Amen.

The Great Explorers

(PROVERBS 25:2)

DANIEL 9–10
1 JOHN 2:18–29
PROVERBS 25:1–12

*O*h Lord God, how great Your goodness to cover a multitude of wrongs, to wash away sin stains by the blood of Your Son. You are the final judge who can order my life file to be sealed, only to be opened by You at the final judgment. Only You have the right to cover up misdoings. I pray that people in authority will investigate matters with impartiality and punish the guilty. I also ask that they be people of vision, seeking to discover what is true and noble and of good report, whether in government, the arts, the sciences, or any matter brought to their attention. Amen.

Lavished in Love
(1 JOHN 3:1–3)

*H*eavenly Father, what honey-coated, life-enhancing, life-giving words these are. You have lavished Your love on me. You spread it extravagantly, not withholding a drop. You called me Your child. I am Yours, in word and deed. In some ways, I am still in a chrysalis. I don't understand what I will one day be, when I am like Christ at His appearing. The more I see of You, the more like You I become. The more I follow You, the more I seek purity. Wrap me in the brilliance of Your light and love until I am changed into the image of Your Son. Amen.

Day 344

Fear Can Be Good

(HOSEA 2:20–3:5)

HOSEA 1–3
1 JOHN 3:13–4:16
PROVERBS 25:18–28

Jesus, my Bridegroom, You called me first and second, and You continue calling me. May I reply with swiftest breath. You are my God. You have planted me, watering me with hope so I in turn can point others to You, the source of eternal life. Even when I'm suffering, I take comfort knowing You chasten me to bring me back more in love with You than before. You give me ears more attuned to understanding and accepting Your loving-kindness. Reverence for and fear of You go hand in hand with comprehending Your care. How wonderful, that the greater my fear of You, so also the greater my understanding of Your love. Amen.

Seeking God
(Hosea 6)

Seeking God, help me to seek You. Stretch my devotion from predawn dew to a daylong, lifelong affair that will last throughout eternity. Not because I'm steadfast, but because that's how much You love me. I want to know more and more of You. The more I learn, the more I want to know. I live in Your hope. If today I feel cut up and wounded, I wait for You, seeking You, knowing You are near. I acknowledge the little I know of You, and I look forward to the day when I shall see You as You are. What a glorious future is mine. Amen.

Day 346

Plowing for Righteousness
(HOSEA 10:11–12)

HOSEA 7–10

2 JOHN

PROVERBS 26:17–21

*M*y True North, keep me centered on You, not whipped around by the hurricane of my own desires. Put a harness on me and put me to work in Your fields. I want to work by Your side, digging in earth that is ready. I'm not sure what a harvest of righteousness looks like, but I trust the crop to You. With Your Spirit moving through me, may I plow straight furrows with right living, acceptance, and rejoicing. Break up the hardness of my heart. Fertilize it with Your unfailing love. Oh Lord, may righteous crops spring forth to Your name. Amen.

Praying for Friends
(3 JOHN)

*L*ord God, I love this friendly little letter from John to a Gentile believer. What a Roman-sounding name, Gaius, along with the Greek-sounding Demetrius, testifying to the radical transformation from a primarily Jewish gathering to a very mixed church unified in You. John's prayer for Gaius sounds like my short prayers when I think of friends: . . .*that they may enjoy good health and that all may go well.* Sometimes I castigate myself for such general prayers, but now I discover I am following the apostle's example. I also pray that their souls get along well as they continue to walk in the truth. May I be faithful in praying for my friends in matters large and small. Amen.

Day 348

Prayer for Revival
(JOEL 1:14)

JOEL 1:1–2:17
JUDE
PROVERBS 27:10–17

*K*ing of kings, I thank You that history doesn't occur in a vacuum, that it began at creation and will continue until everyone bows at Your feet on that great and terrible day of the Lord. I add my voice to those praying for national revival. May a whole host of believers bow before You in repentance. We humbly ask that You will pour out Your Spirit across our nation. Bring back those who have forsaken their roots. May the wonders of Your salvation be heard in every home, by listening hearts. Loose the shackles of our preconceptions until we hear as if for the first time, clearly and without excuse. Amen.

Forsaking My First Love
(REVELATION 2:1–4)

JOEL 2:18–3:21
REVELATION 1:1–2:11
PROVERBS 27:18–27

Head of Your body, the church, You walk among us, watching, knowing us, studying our habits. Forgive us for not being aware of Your presence. I confess I am like Ephesus. I don't really remember that first love; I've been a Christian nearly all my life. When I search those pockets of memory, I recall how happy I was to take my place among the body of believers, to have a family that has been more wonderful than I could have ever imagined. I also remember feeling cleansed, renewed, free. May I recall those gifts of family and cleansing always with the rejoicing of a newborn child. Amen.

Day 350

Amos 1:1–4:5

Revelation 2:12–29

Proverbs 28:1–8

Roaring Lion
(Proverbs 28:1)

Lord God, however bullies see themselves, they are made of straw, easily destroyed by wind or fire. I'm supposed to be a lion, my head covered with Your glory, my voice full of powerful praise, that I may lift my countenance to the rising sun and proclaim Your wonders. May I stand up to my enemies, whether humans or circumstances, with the skill of the lioness. May I walk without fear among my peers and instill an appropriate sense of self in my pride, in my family. May I accept the leadership of the Lion of Judah in all areas of my life. Amen.

Cravings
(Amos 5:14–15)

Amos 4:6–6:14
Revelation 3
Proverbs 28:9–16

Lord God Almighty, thank You for Your Word that shows me that people have always had the same troubles. You offered me a feast of unimaginable riches, but I turned up my nose at it. My hunger has led me to unhealthy, wicked things. I ignore You, when You are my friend—my best friend, in fact. Oh Lord, forgive me. Take what I crave from me, and let me find relief from my withdrawal cravings in You. Continue to mold my heart like Yours, that I will hate evil and love good, shun the one and cling to the other. Amen.

Day 352

Restored
(AMOS 9:14–15)

AMOS 7–9
REVELATION 4:1–5:5
PROVERBS 28:17–24

*M*y Lord God, You have chastened me, burning away my impurities, and now You swoop in and restore to full beauty and function all that has been destroyed in my life. You don't just replace what was lost; You give me something better. You rebuild ruins, replant gardens, and tend vines in Your vineyard. You've grafted me onto Your vine. The graft has taken; I'm tasting of Your life-giving water. Teach me to depend on You in order for Your Spirit to run through me, strengthening body and soul and spirit to do Your will. Amen.

Staying Straight
(Obadiah 1)

OBADIAH–JONAH
REVELATION 5:6–14
PROVERBS 28:25–28

*L*ord God Almighty, whom I'm privileged to call Father, You promise to deliver me, and You do deliver me out of all my troubles. Keep me from repeating the same mistakes. When You rescue me, You offer me so much more. You cleanse me and make me holy, a vessel ready for use. And You will return my inheritance for me to multiply for Your service and glory. May I turn it back into zealous hunger for more of You and for spreading the Gospel. May I accept and act on Your deliverance as a new beginning. Amen.

Day 354

MICAH 1:1–4:5
REVELATION 6:1–7:8
PROVERBS 29:1–8

Where's Dan?

(REVELATION 7:4–8)

*L*ord God, I read the tribes who are numbered among the 144,000 witnesses and wonder why Dan isn't included. It's another reminder that You are sovereign. I can guess at reasons, but I don't need to know the answer, do I? I only need to trust the who—You! You have appointed the right witnesses to Your truth in that coming future time. Just as today You have placed me in this nursing home while my college roommate teaches the Bible in a public setting. I write stories while my son speaks Your truth to unbelievers. You know how and where we best serve, and I trust Your placement. Amen.

God's Requirements
(MICAH 6:8)

*L*ord God Almighty, how much time do I waste when I ask myself what You want me to do? You have made it abundantly clear, over and over again. You don't ask for some terrible sacrifice, or even the ordained sacrifices under the Law. Something comes before wondering whom I should marry or what career path I should follow. You mostly want me to make the right daily choices that lead to the bigger choices. It's in how I choose to treat my neighbor and how closely I follow You as my role model. It's in how much credit I claim for myself and how much praise I turn back to You. If I act justly, love mercy, and walk humbly, I will please You. Amen.

Day 356

No In-Between
(Nahum 1)

NAHUM

REVELATION 9–10

PROVERBS 29:15–23

*G*od of the heavenly armies, there is no in-between with You. I'm either in Your refuge, protected by the shelter of Your wings, or else I'm against You, with the full fury of Your anger falling on me. How thankful I am that Your goodness falls on me. How great Your goodness! How I rejoice in Your shelter, where You have hidden me during bouts of grief, turmoil, and ill health. You care for me, in that You love me. You also take care of me, providing for my every need, keeping me safe from harm in the midst of battle. Amen.

Even When
(Habakkuk 3:17–19)

Habakkuk
Revelation 11
Proverbs 29:24–27

My Savior and my Lord, I've often camped at Habakkuk's prayer. Your goodness, love, and mercy don't change when my circumstances do. That's why I sing when the things I've planted don't bear fruit. When my surroundings are stripped of signs of life and hope, I still rejoice in You. You are my Savior. You are my strength. You give power to the muscles of my faith so that my quivering soul can climb on mountaintops. From there, I get a better perspective. Whether in the valley or on the heights, may I praise You with everything in me. Amen.

Singing Over Me with Love
(ZEPHANIAH 3:17)

ZEPHANIAH
REVELATION 12
PROVERBS 30:1–6

*L*ord God, I cannot escape Your presence. You accompany me everywhere I go. You are mighty with the power to save and also a warrior who fights for me. You care about me that much. You take delight in me—in me, as poor as I am! You rejoice over me, singing love melodies and songs of celebration. You are great, and greatly to be praised! With a God like that, I don't need to fear anything. Your powerful presence gives strength to my arms, that I might join the battle at Your side. If that weren't enough, You restore honor and praise to me, although I'm unworthy of either. May all the glory be returned to You, Lord! Amen.

On a Continuum
(Haggai 2)

*L*ord God, Haggai points back to the day the Israelites left Egypt and forward to Jesus' return as Your signet ring. Your promise doesn't change, and in some ways, past and present are the same to You. You're not bound by time; You created it. Whatever I see around me now, a glorious future awaits me in heaven. Eternal peace awaits me. All the gold and silver, everything I strive for now, belongs to You. I pray that I will strive to fill my heavenly accounts with kingdom currency that I may offer at Your feet. May I gladly share the good news of Your salvation, help when there is a need, and spend my life in Your service. Amen.

Day 360

Praise in Tribulation
(Revelation 15:2–4)

ZECHARIAH 1–4
REV. 14:14–16:3
PROVERBS 30:17–20

*L*ord God Almighty, how much more do I praise You in times of trouble, like the saints of the tribulation? I marvel at Your deeds. They are great and beyond understanding. Your ways steer a straight path, showing no favoritism but delivering a just and fair verdict. You are the ultimate judge of truth. You see all things, even the intents and purposes of the heart. And that's not just true for me and my community, but also for all people in every nation. You alone are holy! No other god worshipped under heaven comes close to measuring up to You. Glory to Your name. Amen.

Beyond the Good Old Days
(ZECHARIAH 8)

ZECHARIAH 5–8
REVELATION 16:4–21
PROVERBS 30:21–28

*L*ord God, I read these verses like I'm longing for the good old days, when the elderly stayed at home and children played in the streets. But You promise so much more than restoration. I am one of Your people because You are my God. You are faithful to me. To me! I have done nothing to deserve Your faithfulness, but that's kind of the point. May I respond in ways pleasing to You. May I do the work You have placed in my hands. Let me speak, judge, and live in truth. Forgive me when I tear others down instead of building them up. May I be part of a swelling throng that is gathering before Your throne to praise You. Amen.

Hope's Prison

(ZECHARIAH 9:12)

ZECHARIAH 9–11

REV. 17:1–18:8

PROVERBS 30:29–33

Oh God who frees me, there's one prison I never want to escape: Your fortress of hope. How blessed I am to dwell in that place where intangible evidence of what is promised is seen as tangible. If I must wear tinted glasses, may they be colored with the golden glory of Your kingdom, blinding me to doubts. Within the walls of my cell, my world expands. I see life through Your eyes, not only today and in my town but also across the miles and through the centuries. You not only restore the past; You also multiply it—twice, ten times, even a hundredfold. Make it so, to Your honor and glory. Amen.

Raise Up Advocates
(Proverbs 31:4–9)

Zechariah 12–14
Revelation 18:9–24
Proverbs 31:1–9

*L*ord of lords, let this be my passion, that I will speak up for those who can't speak for themselves, especially in the nursing home where I live. There are so many people groups who need advocates. Let each person speak as You lead. I pray for city, state, and national leaders, that they won't disobey the law or deny anyone's rights. When there is a conflict of conscience, give them wisdom to know how and when to fight for change. I pray also for their courage and discernment to defend the poor and judge the needy fairly, without political bias. Amen.

Day 364

Divorce
(MALACHI 2:16)

MALACHI 1–2
REVELATION 19–20
PROVERBS 31:10–17

*L*ord of hosts, I feel the depth of Your passion when You say, "I hate divorce" (Malachi 2:16 NASB). I hate it too, but I'm a child of divorce and divorced myself. I thank You for Your forgiveness, grace, and second chances. I pray for my son, for friends and church leaders, that their marriages will be strong. May husbands and wives stand guard against things that will tear their marriages apart. Keep them pure sexually. Let both parties protect their marriage as they would protect their own lives, and together, may they raise children who honor You. I also pray for healing for those who are divorced and for their children. Amen.

Coming Home

MALACHI 3–4
REVELATION 21–22
PROVERBS 31:18–31

Spirit, You called, "Come!" And I have responded, "I am coming." Let me repeat the offer of Your free gift of the water of life to all who thirst. On that day, when the Alpha and Omega closes the door to human history and the bright Morning Star provides all the light needed in His kingdom, I'll be there, by Your grace, because You have made me holy. Just to be there will be glory. Whether my reward is nothing at all or a gold-and-diamond crown, may I throw it at Your feet. Because it's all of You and from You. No more night, no more curse, no more death, no more tears or pain. Hallelujah, amen.

You Might Also Like . . .

Read through the Bible in a Year Journal

This deluxe journal features a plan for reading through the Bible in a year with an accompanying devotional thought inspired by that day's scripture reading. Each entry encourages journalers to read a passage from the Old Testament, New Testament, Psalms, and Proverbs and provides plenty of journaling space for women to record their thoughts and prayers.

Hardback / 978-1-63409-860-1 / $19.99

Secrets of the Proverbs 31 Woman Devotional Journal

This lovely devotional journal, offering equal parts inspiration and encouragement, will uncover the "secrets" of the Proverbs 31 woman. Each reading, tied to a theme from Proverbs 31:10–31, is rooted in biblical truth and spiritual wisdom. Women of all ages will be inspired to emulate the virtues extolled in this memorable passage of scripture.

Hardback / 978-1-68322-554-6 / $19.99